The Fortunate Few

Daniel Lavigne & Carole Drouin

© 2014 Daniel Lavigne and Carole Drouin

All rights reserved. No part of this publication may be reproduced or transmitted in any form or by any means, electronic or mechanical, including photocopying, recording or in any information storage and retrieval system, without permission in writing from the publisher.

Published and distributed by
ImageEtc.
Richmond Hill, Ontario
contact@thefortunatefew.com

Although the authors have exhaustively researched available sources to ensure the accuracy and completeness of the information contained in this book, we assume no responsibility for errors, inaccuracies, omissions or inconsistencies herein. Any slights of people or organizations are unintentional. Readers should use their own judgment and consult financial and legal experts for specific applications to their individual situations.

ISBN 978-0-9939298-1-6

Editor: Donna Dawson, CPE
Cover design: killercovers.com
Page composition: jlmstudio.com

To order more copies of *The Fortunate Few*, visit *TheFortunateFew.com.*

This book is dedicated to everyone
who wants more out of life,
to those who wish to attain their goals
and to those who aspire
to be all they can be.

We thank our parents,

Jeannot Lavigne

Denise Carrière Lavigne

Robert Drouin

Liette Labonté Drouin

and our siblings

for the love and support you've always shown,
and our son, Corey: you are the light of our lives
and you inspire us every day.

Contents

About Us 6

Preface 12
Free from the Alarm Clock: A Typical Day

Chapter 1 22
It Begins with the Way You Think

Chapter 2 46
Assessing Your Relationship with Money

Chapter 3 64
Time Management and Planning

Chapter 4 90
Surround Yourself with Experts: Build Your Team

Chapter 5 104
How We Did It: The Winning Formula

Chapter 6 118
Equity Is Power: Build It and Invest

Chapter 7 132
Budgeting

Chapter 8 144
Saving

Chapter 9 162
Investing

Summary 180

References 188

Acknowledgements 190

About Us

The first step toward success is taken when you refuse to be a captive of the environment in which you first find yourself.

Mark Caine

About Us

"Farniente land," Cayo Coco, Cuba

Cayo Coco, a breathtaking island off the coast of Cuba, is one of the fascinating cays in the Sabana-Camagüey Archipelago. Tourism in the area has increased since a massive causeway was built over marshy land to connect Cayo Coco to mainland Cuba. But we knew we were heading to "farniente (lazy) land," a place that offers a magnificent stretch of white sand beach, still in pristine condition.

After a few days of exploration, we found a group of small huts at one of the extremities of the beach – it was out of our way and quite a distance to walk but we were spellbound by the quiet and the beauty of the area. Two lounge chairs fit in our shelter and we spent our days swimming in the sun and then resting or sleeping in our hut. It was magical. A river cut across the beach a few feet away and it was interesting to see all the tiny fish swimming away from their birthplace, from the fresh water of that riverbed, into the ocean. The needle fish were especially funny: if we stayed still, they would come right up to us, with their long, pointed noses and big protruding eyes. They are curious and congregated around our bodies, skimming the surface in the clear blue ocean.

We stayed there, lounging in our hut, until the sun disappeared and our skin had taken on a golden tone. We had allowed our minds to escape reality and be in the moment. We were connected with nature and our surroundings, really feeling at peace and enjoying each other's touch and love. There is no way to describe how truly blissful these moments can be until you experience them for yourself. We had lots to learn in Cayo Coco, especially about the difference between our wants and our needs and the value of money in a country where life is not based on commercialization.

About Us

Our hut, Cayo Coco, Cuba.

About Us

Cuba to us reflects the state of mind and lifestyle we have been able to attain after 10 short years of disciplined work on our life plan: the enjoyment of being away, discovering new environments and fully appreciating each moment together. We are now financially free and able to choose how we spend our time and where and when we travel. We were not born into wealthy families – but we were willing to commit to a vision and a plan. Here's more on our background. Perhaps you will recognize elements of yourself in our personal journey.

About Us

Daniel

I was raised in the beautiful Niagara Peninsula in Southern Ontario. I graduated from Niagara College with diplomas in business and computer science. My career began at the Welland General Hospital as environmental services supervisor; I later became quality assurance and risk manager.

I later lived in Arizona and California on a three-year working visa. After winning the Mr. North America title – a first for a Canadian – I was sponsored by a well-known American modelling agency. That chapter of my life is filled with interesting stories. I then returned to Canada to start a new career in computer technology with a French school board in Toronto. I also mastered the art of negotiating a deal as a real estate investor, as well as public speaking. I genuinely believe that a comprehensive education must include financial literacy. Set your goals, make a plan, stay focused and execute it. Remember, "if it's going to be, it's up to me."

I had planned an early retirement for quite some time – I always wanted a life of freedom and adventure with the love of my life. I wanted that freedom while I was still healthy, with plenty of endurance and stamina to tackle all the adventures I desired. I ended my full-time work career at age 46. Strangely enough, it happened to be on the last day of the Mayan Calendar, December 21, 2012. I had not planned it that way but that coincidence brought some attention to my retirement and I was invited to do a radio interview for the Canadian Broadcasting Corporation to discuss how I achieved such an early retirement. I had colleagues say I would enjoy just one day of freedom because the world was coming to an end! Needless to say, we're still here and I feel very fortunate that life as we know it continues.

Carole

I am from Clarence Creek, located in the rural French county of Prescott-Russell, near Ottawa, Ontario. I graduated from the University of Ottawa with degrees in criminology and leisure science. I moved to Vancouver, where I completed a certification in business communication at Simon Fraser University.

About Us

After 10 years in Vancouver, I moved to Toronto and completed an executive Master of Business Administration degree, sponsored by the Toronto Board of Trade. I served as a strategic communications advisor to public service leaders ranging from school board executives to provincial cabinet ministers.

I have dedicated my passion to the cause of French-language minorities across Canada. I was responsible for communications with the Fédération des francophones de la Colombie-Britannique, with British Columbia's first French-language school board, with one the largest French-language school boards in Ontario (in Toronto) and with the Minister of Francophone Affairs. For six years I served as executive director of the French Catholic School Trustees Association, a strategic and political lobby group within the Ontario education system. I have also trained spokespersons in public relations.

I quit my job in November 2012, almost two months before Daniel's retirement. It remains a joke between us that I retired before he did, at age 45. I had never imagined in my wildest dreams being able to experience such freedom so early in life. I remember thinking when I was very young, listening to my dad during his morning routine, that I'd never be able to make it through high school, and university, and then dozens of years of waking up that early to get to work – especially during the winter. Later, during my teenage years, I thought it unfair that we had to spend the "best years" of our lives studying or working, with very little vacation time and not much money. Freedom, it seemed, came only much later in life. That was until I met Daniel and we set out a plan to take control of our lives and make sense of what we really wanted to accomplish in life.

We proved to be a great team, running a successful business purchasing and renting real estate while attaining financial freedom. We co-founded online-homes.net in 2004. We are really just two average Canadians who fell in love and wanted to live their dreams. Through this book, we will share how we accomplished our goals and achieved financial freedom.

We live in Richmond Hill, Ontario, and spend winters in Costa Rica. We have one son, Corey.

Preface
Free from the Alarm Clock:
A Typical Day

Time is free, but it's priceless. You can't own it, but you can use it.
You can't keep it, but you can spend it.
Once you've lost it you can never get it back.

Harvey MacKay

Treehouse adventure, Costa Rica

The community of Finca Bellavista is named after Rio Bellavista, a river that flows through the middle of the village, and for the incredible beauty of the surroundings and the bountiful flora and fauna. Finca Bellavista is a residential treehouse community on the southern Pacific Coast region of Costa Rica. It is rustic, yet has the comforts of home: running water, kitchen, bathroom and even a shower, all in a tree.

We decided to live a four-day experience in this private retreat off the beaten path to explore the natural wonders of the rainforest canopy and enjoy trees, plants, wildlife and fresh air. It is not a full-service spa or a fancy hotel; it's really about connecting with nature and getting in touch with yourself. It's about removing yourself from your day-to-day reality and experiencing something new.

We swam under a waterfall and down a river, relaxed in natural river pods, zip-lined and most importantly, lived in a tree! Walking the surrounding trails we encountered suspension bridges over pristine river canyons. We even saw a sloth slowly moving along a large branch and heard its whistle-like call. It was truly spectacular. We met a man in the process of building his own treehouse, a two-level home suspended high up in a tree. He was proud to walk us through it, explaining how his lifelong dream was becoming a reality.

Finca Bellavista encompasses over 600 acres of rainforest and pastures. Some treehouses are perched above the Golfo Dulce and nurtured by two white-water rivers. The location of this unique enclave is unmatched in its magnificence and it pulses with life. When we left Finca Bellavista we left rejuvenated. It was an unforgettable life-changing experience.

Preface

Below our tree house, Finca Bellavista, Costa Rica.

14

We love to reminisce about our stay in the treehouse – it is one of our most adventurous trips so far. What's more, we met the young couple who developed this project, a truly inspiring encounter. They left life as they knew it back in Colorado after travelling to Costa Rica and vowing to protect this rainforest from being destroyed by development. They risked all they had to buy a large piece of that forest to undertake their own project: building a community of houses in those trees to showcase the beauty of the jungle. We felt privileged to be able to experience that deep connection with nature and it reignited that primal need for freedom and space to live life passionately. Freedom here does not mean no work but rather devoting yourselves to something you are passionate about.

Daniel

It's 7:45 AM, but no alarm sounds for us anymore. The birds are chirping loudly, which begins to stimulate my senses. My body and mind start to awaken from a peaceful sleep. The curtains are moving freely in the warm breeze. I open my eyes to see the love of my life peacefully sleeping next to me. I slide against her and give her a gentle kiss on the lips. Then I move back to watch her as she slowly awakens from a deep, calm, stress-free sleep.

What a life we have! How lucky I am to have my love lying next to me. How lucky we are to be living this life of freedom, to do as we wish, to wake up when our bodies and minds wish to.

She opens her eyes and gives me a little smile and says, "Bonjour, mon amour."

"Good morning," I answer, looking into her beautiful face.

Carole

I feel a gentle kiss – much better than an alarm clock. As I stretch and open my eyes, I am amazed at the intensity of the light entering our bedroom. I feel like a princess. Daniel, my prince charming, has the most beautiful blue eyes.

The sun has been up for a while. I am grateful every time I sleep through the night without waking. I never felt this rested when I was working. I would rewrite speeches in my mind, finish up briefs and prepare PowerPoint presentations at 3 AM. None of these monkey-mind activities disturb my sleep now.

Daniel

It is now around 9 AM. Most people are at work now, trying to figure out how to fit everything into their busy schedules. I pour my coffee and as usual, sit on our dock by Lake Wilcox, reading. Two Mallard ducks come to greet me. I see Carole come out the patio door with her coffee in hand. She says, "Another beautiful day." It is always a beautiful day with her in my life; what more could I ask for? The breeze makes her long blonde hair dance gently as she sits next to me. I am living the dream.

My thoughts drift to our to-do list. We make one every day and developing it becomes the basis for deciding how our day will unfold. Do we want to take the motorbike out? Should we do some gardening? Is it time to plan another trip? Shall we go canoeing, kayaking or hiking? Should we work on writing this book? Which of our business obligations shall we tackle? Should we perhaps clean the house? We have always believed in daily to-do lists and have created them religiously all our professional lives and continue to do so. We credit this practice with bringing us the success and freedom we experience today – it keeps us focused, on track and productive. But more on that later.

Carole

As I sit on the dock with Daniel, I think to myself, I used to be the first one up because I needed a bit more time to get ready for work. But now I enjoy stepping out of bed after Daniel. What a joy! Morning is my favourite part of the day, having coffee with that handsome man. Spring is in the air. The Kayak and Canoe Club members are already on the lake training. I would love to make a garden this summer…Maybe we will add this to our to-do list.

Daniel

After reading for 45 minutes I get up and head to the kitchen. I boil water and make us breakfast – oatmeal with fresh cut fruit. I lay the pieces of fruit on top of the oatmeal and top it off with vanilla yogurt. I grab the pot of coffee and make my way back to the dock, where Carole sits reading. I pour her some coffee and put her breakfast in front of her. She looks up at me with that smile and says, "Merci, chéri."

"De rien, mon amour," I answer. She closes her book and we begin discussing the to-do list as we slowly eat our breakfast. "What do you say we go canoeing today, and perhaps this time take a dip?" I suggest.

Preface

"I'd like to fit in some yoga this morning."

"Yoga is a good idea."

"Perhaps a picnic on Toronto Island for lunch afterwards," Carole suggests.

"Should we take the motorbike?"

"They're calling for a nice day so that's a good idea. Tomorrow, rain is in the forecast; perhaps we can do our bookkeeping and answer emails then."

We bounce a few ideas back and forth. Soon, this is what our to-do list for the day looks like:

- Prepare a picnic to go to Toronto Island.
- Put in a load of laundry.
- Do a 45-minute yoga session.
- Pack the motorbike with picnic supplies and head to the Island for the day.
- On the way home, pick up fruit and vegetables at the fruit market.
- Stop by one of our rental homes to inspect an uneven walkway.
- Get home around 5 PM.
- Have a barbecue dinner.
- Fold the laundry and put it away.
- If weather permits and we are lucky enough to have a little wind, do some wind surfing; if not, take the canoe out.
- Practise our rumba for 30 minutes – tomorrow we have a dance lesson.
- Plan a vegetable garden, including choosing the location.

This is a typical to-do list for us now. When we had traditional work careers, we had our personal to-do lists, plus long work lists for both of us – we're pretty sure you're familiar with how long, tedious and tiresome those can get.

Why Us?

Maybe you're wondering whether you can attain this kind of freedom. We believe that with a plan and determination and by following the steps to reach your goals, anyone can achieve success. Why not you? We have always been interested in learning about and from people who live their desired lifestyles. We have read many biographies and often make an effort to meet with those who were willing to share their recipes for success and to talk about their motivation.

If you decide you will take the necessary steps, commit to them and really apply yourself, you can achieve anything. In our opinion, it takes approximately 10 years to become a true professional at what you do. If you keep your focus and are determined to devote your time and energy for at least 10 years, you will achieve your goals. For us, success does not mean only doing well at your job, but also setting up a plan, investing in real estate, investing in yourself, saving and working toward your goals and objectives. A little later we explain in detail how we organized our plan and how we applied it to gain financial freedom, which now allows us to live the lifestyle we desire. We credit our success to planning and to taking action – it takes drive and energy to implement a plan like ours. Let us guide you to wealth and freedom.

Friends, family and colleagues often asked how we were able to retire so young and live this amazing lifestyle. When we explained our approach, some suggested we write a book. So we did just that, recognizing that writing a book, coupled with developing a website, would be a great way to help others achieve financial freedom like we did.

Preface

This book offers insight into our own journey to financial independence. None of the content, data, analysis, anecdotes or recollections contained in this book should be construed as investment or lifestyle advice – the products and services we have chosen to use and the lifestyle we have pursued relate to our specific circumstances and may not work for you. You should speak with your own accountant and financial advisors, study investing and get professional advice about the risks of all financial products. This book represents our personal journey and opinions and should be enjoyed as such.

We came up with the title of the book this way: A very good friend, James, brought together those who meant the most to him so they could meet. James came up with the Fortunate Few as a name for that select group. This group has now been in existence for many years. Laughter, stories and fun are part of every meeting. How fortunate we feel to be part of it – yet we were all strangers before James brought us together. We hope you will feel like one of the fortunate few after reading our book.

To our family, friends, acquaintances, colleagues and those reading this book, welcome to *The Fortunate Few*. Good luck on your journey!

Chapter 1
It Begins
with the Way You
Think

*We cannot solve our problems with the same thinking
we used when we created them.*

Albert Einstein

Riding the wave, Las Catalinas, Costa Rica

Daniel

The beach town of Las Catalinas is only 15 minutes from our house in Costa Rica and we were told it is beautiful. So off we went! We got on our motorbike and drove through the village of Potrero and along a mountainside. The smell of the sea was refreshing and we were offered an amazing view. When we got to the top, yet another spectacular view awaited.

Las Catalinas is also the name of a set of small islands approximately 10 kilometres offshore; it's known as one of the best spots to scuba dive in all of Costa Rica. The surrounding waters are home to giant mantas, sea turtles, eels and huge schools of fish, among other marine life.

As we stood there, we looked at each other and said, "Kayaking?" at the same time. "Let's do it!" Soon enough we were at sea in our kayaks. We were instructed to paddle out toward the islands and then north along the shore to a remote white sand beach. While we were heading off toward these spectacular islands we were excited to see sting rays jumping out of the water and flying. There must have been 20 of them. It was one of the most amazing things we had ever witnessed.

We continued our adventure heading south, observing the shoreline and a beach that looked like an oasis. We were simply enjoying ourselves, talking and slowly paddling. Carole, floating slightly behind me, started yelling like she was being attacked. I quickly looked back to find her approximately five metres above me, riding a large wave. Within seconds, she came crashing down on me and I suddenly found myself spinning under water as if in a washing machine. Fighting to find my way up, I finally got my head above water and heard Carole laughing hysterically. She was swimming toward the beach. I called out, "What about your kayak?"

She could barely answer she was laughing so hard. "The waves will bring it in," she shouted. So I began swimming toward the shore where she now lay, still laughing. I hugged her close, laughing too, and we rolled in the sand like young lovers. After catching our breath, I noticed the kayaks about 10 metres from us, getting hit by the surf. We pulled them up onto the sand and then stood, looking at this amazing, secluded white beach with palm trees shooting toward the blue sky. We spent many hours there before returning our rented kayaks. Staying afloat was our lesson of the day!

Chapter 1

Las Catalinas Islands in the distance, Costa Rica.

As you can see from our Catalinas adventure, we are not experts in sea kayaking! But we did not focus too much on the fear we experienced when that wave took both of us under. We have consciously decided to remain positive, no matter what situation may arise. That positive outlook has to be consciously cultivated because it's human nature to be critical of ourselves and others. This attitude empowers us to move forward, to welcome change as a learning opportunity, and it certainly brings adventure and excitement to our life together.

Chapter 1

Why Wait?

Financial institutions and the media spend millions promoting "retirement" as the ultimate goal of your working life but we believe financial freedom is attainable for younger people. A plan to make this happen in 10 or 15 years is easier to focus on than the traditional retirement, half a century away!

Neuro-Associative Conditioning

Making that plan and achieving that goal begins with changing the way you think. From our perspective, most of our motivations are linked to feelings about a given task and these feelings determine how you measure the effort needed to accomplish that task.

Your perception, or feelings, determine your level of ambition, determination, motivation and desire to succeed. The stronger your feelings, the greater your determination, motivation and desire. Isn't this what passion is all about? This applies to all aspects of your life, including how you relate to love, work, food, exercise – everything. If you associate eating ice cream with pain, it may be because you associate it with gaining weight. If you have negative feelings about it, you are not likely going to eat it very often. But if you associate eating ice cream with pleasure, you are likely to eat more of it. Similarly, your feelings toward your goals, positive or negative, will determine your level of determination and achievement.

What we just described is known as neuro-associative conditioning, a scientific approach to self-conditioning and change in human beings developed by Anthony Robbins, author of *Unlimited Power*, *Awaken the Giant Within* and the *Personal Power* series. It is based on the premise that there are two determining reasons for human behaviour: the need to avoid pain and the desire to feel pleasure. These neuro-associations are the directing force of all human behaviour.

Anything you set out to achieve is based on how you relate to pleasure and pain. For example, if you say, "I plan to own five properties" and then you associate pain with all the work involved, including dealing with discontented tenants, your chances of achieving that goal are next to none. You will not have the drive or the desire to invest the effort needed to achieve it. On the other hand, if you associate the pleasure of financial satisfaction with owning the properties, you will have the motivation and determination to achieve that goal.

Here's another example. If you set out to lose 20 pounds in one year, but think of the pain of having to exercise, imagine that you need to starve yourself or think you will not be able to join your co-workers at restaurants or the kids for ice cream, you are bound not to lose the weight because you have associated that goal with pain. If you instead associate your weight loss with pleasure by visualizing how good you will look and how amazing you will feel and by knowing you will be healthy and will set a great example for your kids, being in control of what you eat, then you are well on your way to achieving your goal.

Neuro-cognitive association also works if you are seeking new employment: think of the search for a new job as a positive learning experience. With every rejection you receive, you are getting closer in finding the employer that will hire you. If you associate your job search with the pain of rejection and failure, you will sabotage your efforts to attain the job you desire.

It's a simple approach and it applies to everything in your life: learning to play an instrument or speak a language, getting your finances in order or attaining health goals. It all depends on whether you associate what you have to do with pleasure or pain. Once you understand this and realize you can control your outlook on life – that is, you can associate anything with pain or pleasure – you can achieve anything you consciously set out to do.

Chapter 1

Procrastination:
Avoiding Decision-Making and Change

What neuro-cognitive association really means is that it's possible to break free from bad decisions and from being trapped inside familiar parameters by changing the way you think about things. Step out of your comfort zone and stop procrastinating. Many people say, "I would like that" or "I would like to do this" but never make the decision to actually take action and *do* something about these desires.

We noticed people around us at work believing that if they worked hard on a given task or put a lot of time into something, they were productive. But ask yourself whether whatever you are doing is really worthwhile. Is the task part of *your* plan? Being able to identify whether that work is really worth it is a major part of being successful – meaning it brings you closer to your goals and aspirations, to getting what *you* desire in life.

Many people respond to that approach by saying, "You don't understand my position, you're not in my shoes." But you are in the position you are in because you put yourself there or allow yourself to stay in that situation. We know there are exceptions, but in most cases you are where you are because of the decisions you have made. You need to decide where you really want to be. In most cases the solution is quite simple.

But watch out for the ego, your sense of self-esteem or self-importance. As a sense of self-identity develops over time from past experiences and what you have learned, your ego helps make you who you are. We are not born with an ego. Our egos help us maintain a certain balance, like a rider on a horse. The rider knows where they're going and has determined that destination. The horse also has a mind of its own and will sometimes take a different path. The rider continues to adjust the reins, guiding the horse to the rider's choice of path. Like the rider on the horse, we sometimes find ourselves going in directions chosen by our ego and struggling to stay on the path we have chosen to get to our goal.

It Begins with the Way You Think

Your ego is an image or a representation you have of yourself, but sometimes it doesn't reflect your true self. We can better ourselves by going beyond our egos to become self-aware and pull the reins when the ego tries to take control. Being connected to your inner self, being aware of our inner thoughts, emotions and feelings, is an important part of knowing yourself and making decisions that feel right. When you dominate your ego, you are acting as your true self. Sometimes, you may believe your ego is well under control and that you know how to tame it, but it may still interfere in your decision-making. Learn to recognize when it is time to move on or break away from your old ways, your pre-conceived ideas, your beliefs and your habits, even if your ego tells you to stay because it's comfortable.

Often people get caught up in the emotional side of a situation, which makes it seem like a big deal even when it's not. When you look back at situations that preoccupied you or bothered you 10 years ago you may say to yourself, "My God, it seemed like such a big deal at the time! We were so melodramatic, when really, it was easy to fix." Remember the first time you wanted to jump off a cliff into the water below as a thrill? It may have taken you 30 minutes to finally do it, but once you did it, you realized it was easy – there was nothing to it. Once in the water below, looking up, it did not seem all that high after all.

Most problems we face today are the same. We have had people tell us their problems and sometimes we can't believe how simple it would be to fix them. One said, "I can't make ends meet." We looked at their finances and simply removed the entertainment package they had chosen for their TV viewing and cut out restaurant meals – they're now back on track.

Another person said, "I hate my boss!" We said, "Request a transfer to another department."

"I hate my job!" "Get a different job."

"I'm broke." "Get a better job, or get a second job."

Chapter 1

"I don't have the skills to get a better job." "Go to school in the evenings."

"I have no money for my retirement." "Start saving now."

"I have no time for myself." "Stop wasting so much time whining!"

If and when you fail, or discover you have wasted your time at something, look at it as a lesson. Don't repeat the same actions. The person who told us she hates her job but stayed with it made the conscious choice to continue punishing herself. Stop procrastinating and take the steps necessary to change your circumstances. There is always a solution within you.

We were in a bad situation with our boss when we worked at the same employer. Our boss was given a lot of responsibility in the organization and, unfortunately, was a classic bully. We had two options: find new jobs, like 16 other people did because of him, or do what felt right and bring him to leave the organization. We made the decision that we were going to attempt to have him removed with the help of a few colleagues who felt the same way. Two years later, he was gone. We exposed his behaviour by recording each meeting with him and sending the recordings to the president of the organization. Once she had proof of our complaints, she fired him. This was a difficult time for our colleagues and for us but we had decided to do something to change a bad situation. We did risk losing our jobs and emotions ran high, but we were convinced we were making the right decision. Once we stepped into our action plan nothing could stop us.

The decision to act, to do something, is a choice. Ignoring a bad situation and refusing to provoke change is a refusal to take control of your destiny, to take matters into your own hands and make positive choices. This is true at work or in a relationship. These are difficult decisions – emotions are involved. But relationships are an important learning ground, especially for learning about yourself. Don't settle for less at work or in a relationship when you know it's not what your heart aspires to; find the essential qualities you seek.

If you are not in a good relationship, do yourself a favour and fix it or call it off. How many people look back years later and say, "Why did I not do it sooner?"

We have the greatest appreciation for the wisdom of Jim, one of Daniel's best friends. Daniel, at age 25, had just moved to California and was going through major life changes. Jim, already retired and in his 60s, often asked Daniel if he was happy. Then one day, Daniel asked him, "Are *you* happy?" Jim's surprising answer was "No." He then explained that he had been living with a woman he did not love for over 40 years. He said, "Daniel, I don't want you to make the same mistake. We are here on Earth for a very short time. Live it, make the right decisions." It saddened Daniel to know Jim had lived much of his life feeling unhappy, even after having children and a successful career.

Daniel asked him if he had ever been in love. Jim said, "Yes, and I still love her." He had fallen in love with a woman in Croatia when he was young and had managed to see her five or six times during his life, allowing that love to take over their lives for a short time. He and the woman confessed their love to each other in their 60s, acknowledging they had made the wrong decisions and that they should have spent their lives together.

Jim opened Daniel's eyes, offering his perspective on life and on Daniel's own tribulations. People who are fortunate to live to an old age have a lot of wisdom to offer. Some bear many regrets. We have a lot to learn from them.

Any relationship separation is likely to cause a financial setback. You may think it might be easier to stay in the relationship, dealing with the families, the drama – the children especially. Is that the easy way out? How do we make the right decision when it comes to relationships? Why not stick to it for the long run? Relationships are never clear cut, but at the same time, being with the right partner is a question that needs to be addressed if you are serious about achieving your goals, be they financial freedom or other types of success. We have each other and our life together is wonderful and satisfying.

Chapter 1

Do You Know What You Want out of Life? Assess Your Drive!

Having drive and a desire to get more out of life is a must to give you the ambition and determination to reach the goals you long for. That drive is the fuel on your journey to reach your destination. If you are content with your life as it is and have no unachieved goals or aspirations, if you do not have feelings of need or want, you won't have the drive or ambition for more because you don't need it.

Understanding your own values is part of the awareness you have to develop when you reflect on what you need and want out of life (books have been written on this subject). We all have different values – some we inherit from our parents and some find their place in our souls as we evolve through life. Some people feel contentment and satisfaction with where they are, whereas others would never settle for "so little." For some, providing for their family and being present for their partners and children is their ultimate goal. They may still be working toward this goal, but if they have attained it then they have succeeded. For some it isn't about discovering the world, going on a mission in a developing country or having more money or their own business.

But those who are striving for more or who have different aspirations in life must change the way they think. They must understand that the neuro-associations relating to that "want" will increase or decrease their drive in pursuing that goal.

> *Daniel: Once you hit rock bottom, the only way to go is up*

After I won an international competition that my first wife had registered me for – believe it or not, the Mr. North America title – many opportunities arose. As one of the prizes, I was awarded a contract with the Ford/Robert Black Modeling Agency, which sponsored me in the United States through a program to model and act. So off I went, leaving a great job and going into the unknown!

I quickly learned what being a starving actor meant. I also quickly learned that I was a terrible actor and that the people I was competing with had many years of acting experience and training. I came to hate my life and what I had become, although I have no regrets because these experiences served as a lifelong lesson. I literally was starving and I felt I was taking advantage of people around me for lodging and food, just surviving day to day. I loved Arizona and California but again, decisions came into play; I had to stop procrastinating. I missed my son and the professional life and stability I had enjoyed when I worked for the Welland County General Hospital as quality assurance and risk manager. What was I accomplishing in California? Obviously, I had to break from that situation.

I opted for a major career change and on my return to Ontario I went into information technology as a network administrator. With no experience, I decided I would take the Microsoft Certified Systems Engineer program. A friend of my father told him I would never pass this intense course because I had no experience with computers, and that even if I obtained the certificate, it would take me 10 years to become a network administrator. Moreover, at that time I was a one-finger typist!

My father took a risk by sharing this prediction with me – it could have discouraged me. But my father knew me well, and it did just the opposite. I took the challenge and worked as hard as I possibly could. I obtained my MCSE status and within a year, was working for the French Catholic School Board as systems administrator. Within five years I supervised a team of 13 technicians.

I am telling you this with humility, to impress upon you how quickly things can change in your life if you make strong decisions. With determination and persistence you can achieve whatever you want. But it all starts with the decision, followed by planning, which we'll talk about later. Once you start making decisions, you will be on your way to financial independence and you will live a happy and prosperous life.

Many people will accomplish more in their lives with less talent, education and ability than you have. How? Many have left their re-

Chapter 1

lationships or their jobs to take a different direction in life. Millions of people do it every day. You won't be alone; you won't die from making tough decisions. Once you assess your situation and start planning, a variety of options will present themselves for your consideration. The most important step to financial freedom is making a plan to attain your desired goal. The earlier you start, the younger you will be when you achieve that success.

Carole: Lessons of wisdom

I have pushed my limits throughout my life, venturing to learn more and keep myself challenged. I was born in a very small village of approximately 500 inhabitants about 50 kilometres east of Ottawa, near the Ottawa River. I consider myself very lucky: I had a very happy childhood with wonderful parents, five siblings to play with, fields to run through in the summer, ponds to skate on in the winter and many secret spots for hide-and-seek.

After high school, I attended university in Ottawa and left home at 17 to avoid the daily commute. I was looking forward to independence and taking control of my life. I clearly remember my discussion with Dad, a one-on-one at the dining room table, and the "100 questions" we had to go through whenever a serious issue arose. Well, I had chosen to study criminal law, an unconventional domain for women. My plan was to work with prisoners and improve the rehabilitation system, not to become a lawyer. My dad had lots of questions about my career plan and life plan as I was moving out. But my mind was set, and although I could sense some degree of disagreement from my father, I was assuming all costs for my education and I thought the decision was mine.

I held three part-time jobs throughout my four-year program. I had a busy life and loved it. Although being comfortable with legal jargon has always been useful, I never worked in criminology; my father had a lot of wisdom, and I clearly remember many of the questions he posed to me.

My first job out of university was in communications and was offered to me by one of my professors, who appreciated my writing style. A year later, I decided to test new ground and moved to Vancouver with my boyfriend, whom I ended up marrying. Beautiful BC! My plan was to stay there for a couple of years…which stretched into a decade. I was involved in an organization that lobbied for French education in BC. Once a French-language school authority was created, I was hired to take on its communication department.

I never stayed more than five years with the same employer, a rule I set for myself to keep learning. I moved to Toronto in 2000, lured back to Ontario by a recruiter for another challenge with the French Catholic School Board. During that period, I decided to get my MBA. I also met the man who would propel me into another universe – I fell in love with Daniel like I never thought possible. He quickly became my soul mate, my partner, my best friend and my lover. We shared the same perspective on life and together, we could plan… and fly!

There are no easy big decisions in life – the ones relating to relationships, family and career – but if you remain true to yourself, you can steer in the right direction.

As we were shopping for our first home together, Daniel received an email from his ex-wife in California, suggesting that Corey, their 10-year-old son, could come and live with us. Talk about planetary alignment! We were jumping with joy and overwhelmed by the prospect of building a nest for our newly formed family. Daniel's happiness seemed complete and having a child in my life was a true gift.

I moved on in my career, as set in my long-term plan, and became senior advisor in communications to a provincial cabinet minister. That incursion into politics was fascinating and prepared me for my next challenge as executive director of the organization serving elected trustees of the Ontario French Catholic School Board. I remained in that position for six years before retiring.

When I look back at my life – my career, my family life and my relationships – it's clear that procrastination would have sabotaged my true potential for attaining my lifelong dreams.

Chapter 1

Woulda, Shoulda, Coulda: Changing Your Old Patterns and Beliefs

Start on your path to decision-making by questioning and assessing the perceptions you have about your surroundings. Sometimes our external influences affect our judgment and bring about selective discrimination. At other times, we decide in our minds that something is good or bad without fully understanding it. We need to be open to new ideas.

To illustrate, we would like to introduce you to four individuals: Mr. Shoulda Dunn, Ms. Woulda Iffa, Mr. Coulda Bean and Ms. Didit Wright.

These four people, now in their 40s, had been high school classmates. After planning for four months they were finally able to get together at a café. Didit deserves the credit for making the meeting happen. They had a lot of catching up to do; they hadn't seen each other for 20 years. After the big hugs and hellos they sat down and it was obvious they were happy to see each other again.

Shoulda started the conversation by asking, "Coulda, what are you doing these days"?

Coulda answered, "I'm presently unemployed – I've been looking for work for the last 11 months. I had the opportunity, in my last job, to take some evening courses paid for by my employer – I could've become a certified systems engineer. I could've been working in a position that opened up in the company 14 months ago. But I didn't want to fill up my evenings."

Shoulda said, "That's too bad; you should've taken the opportunity."

Coulda replied, "Yes, I know. I'd be employed today if I had."

Shoulda looked at Didit and asked, "How about you? I heard you were doing quite well."

Didit answered, "Yes, things are going very well. I recently quit my 9-to-5 job and am doing what I want. I have a few little projects on the go. I have a few homes I rent out and I like to keep myself busy by updating and maintaining my properties. Some may call it work but it's what I choose to do so I don't see it that way. It's been a good business for me."

Shoulda jumped in. "Yeah, I should've invested in real estate too."

"I could have but I had kids; the timing was wrong," Coulda said.

Woulda said, "I would've but it's too risky."

Shoulda looked at Didit and asked, "What made you do it?"

"Well," Didit answered, "I wanted to retire early. So I planned for it and made sure I executed that plan."

Shoulda quickly interjected and said, "Yeah, I should've done that too, but it's too late now…"

Didit interrupted, "No, it's never too late!"

Woulda then said, "I would've but my husband didn't see things the same way I did and would never take that kind of risk."

Coulda asked Didit, "How about your family life – how's that going?"

Didit replied, "Couldn't be happier. My daughter is finishing her fifth year of university, in dentistry. My son is completing a three-year business program. They both live close to their universities. My husband, Done-That, is also retired so we spend a lot of time travelling. We are very happy and feel very fortunate."

Shoulda said, "I should've travelled when I had the chance. I can't afford it now."

Just then a young woman approached the table and said, "Hi, Mom!"

Woulda looked up and answered, "Hi, sweetheart." She looked at her old classmates and said, "This is my daughter, Poorme." Gesturing toward her friends she continued, "These are the friends I told

Chapter 1

you about. Please meet Shoulda, Coulda and Didit."

Didit said, "Pull up a chair and join us." Poorme sat down and Didit asked, "So Poorme, what do you do?"

Poorme replied, "Well, I graduated from university and am still unemployed. It's so hard nowadays to find work; it's not like in your day when jobs fell in your laps as you graduated. Must be nice. I wish I was born back then."

Didit remained silent. Then Shoulda spoke, looking at Poorme, "Listen, instead of saying how lucky we were, perhaps you should do what I should've done years ago. I should've done what Didit did – plan and work toward my goals. I should have prevented myself from getting in the position I'm stuck in today."

Didit blushed a bit.

Coulda joined in, "Yeah, me too. I could've made better choices in my life. It's easy for us to sit here and say how lucky Didit is, but I could've done it too. I guess I just chose not to."

Woulda then said, "Coulda and Shoulda are right. I would've done things a lot differently if I had known. Now, I hear myself in my daughter. I wish I'd been a better example."

Poorme looked at Didit and said, "How did you become so successful, Didit? How come you are so fortunate?"

Didit said humbly, "Well, I planned, studied and stayed on track. I took steps to ensure I did what I set out to accomplish. If you have the time and patience to listen, I would love to share my story." The others nodded with approval and Woulda ordered another round of coffee. Didit continued. "My husband and I made a plan. We knew exactly what it was we wanted and nothing was going to stop us. We used daily to-do lists that helped keep us on track and achieve our goals. Time flies and we wanted to live life to the fullest. Yes, we quit our jobs – we now own multiple properties and we travel widely. We love our life. I tell you this not to impress you but to impress upon you that you can accomplish whatever you want in life."

Didit addressed Poorme. "You said it's harder to get a job today than it was in our day. I beg to differ. Today, young people have a lot more job opportunities than we ever did. You have the Internet, where you can search for jobs and information on opportunities around the globe. If you compare airfare to average income 20 years ago, it is much more affordable now than it was in our day to travel long distances. My first laptop cost me $5,000! Today, you can get one for a few hundred and it does much more than my old computer could ever do. My kids, who are the same age as you, found jobs without too much trouble."

Poorme countered, "But they are lucky – they have you to help them." She suddenly looked sheepish. "Sorry mom."

Didit asked, "Who paid for your university education?"

"Mom and Dad."

"I did not pay for any of my kids' education. They earned the money to pay for it themselves," Didit said. "My kids worked evening and weekend jobs while they were away at school. One went into a co-op program to help him fund his education. They have been working since they were in their early teens and have impressive resumes. What does your resume look like? How much work experience do you have?"

Poorme thought for a moment, "Well, I babysat and gave some guitar lessons while living with Mom and Dad. That's about it."

Didit sighed. "Listen, I'm not trying to make you feel bad, I'm saying this to help you understand that you need to stop thinking as if you are a victim. Take hold of your life – own it and be responsible for your decisions. As for your comments about how lucky you think I am, here's what you don't know: my first marriage failed. I was unemployed at one point. I lived out of the country for a while and had to build my credit all over again because my Canadian credit rating wasn't recognized." Didit smiled, trying not to seem like she was lecturing. "I'm starting to wish I was born in *your* time!"

Chapter 1

"So before you start judging successful or 'fortunate' people, first appreciate that most of us started exactly where you are today. I have a friend who at your age immigrated to Canada from Italy with $20 in his pocket. I don't think you can say it was easier for him than it is for you today. Poorme, you need to stop making excuses. We all face challenges and need to take steps to move forward. No, I did not always have a good job but I certainly never stayed unemployed. I've even worked parking cars to make ends meet. So if you think it was easy for me and my husband, you're wrong. You need to learn from people like me as I learned from others who attained the lifestyle I wanted."

Didit continued. "Look around this table. Ask Shoulda what he feels he should have done. Ask Coulda what he could have been if he had done things differently. Ask your mother if there's anything she would have done differently. And learn from them. Don't make the same mistakes they made. Educate yourself. Have you ever heard that saying, 'if it's going to be, it's up to me'? No one is going to do it for you." She looked at Woulda. "Parents who don't teach their children to fend for themselves are not doing them any favours. Part of teaching your children is allowing them to make mistakes."

Poorme thought for a moment, then concluded, "As hard as it's been listening to this, what you're saying is true. I know people come from all over the world to live in this country because of the opportunities here, and I'm sitting here saying, 'look at poor little me.' You did it, and you were in a situation that was worse than mine. I'm sorry for assuming that everything was easy for you. You've given me some real insight, Didit – thank you. I think I better go home and make a plan!"

Poorme stood to leave. "It was nice meeting you all. I'm pumped! I realize I'm much better off than many who have become successful. I guess everything *is* possible when you put your mind to it and just *do* it."

She leaned over and kissed her mother on the cheek.

Overcoming Fear

Many people are afraid of stepping out of their comfort zone. For example, people are often hesitant to travel to a new country, change employment, go into business, leave an unhappy marriage, etc. According to research published in *Psychology Today* in 2012, surveys about our fears commonly show fear of public speaking at the top of the list – this fear is so great, it's stronger than the fear of death. Fear of misery or poverty also appears on most lists of top fears, as do fear of rejection, ridicule and loneliness. Fear of the unknown and fear of change are part of the countdown too.

We could spend a lot of time on this subject, but we believe that you just have to push your boundaries. You will find that just like riding a bike, the more you "do it" – pushing your limits and dealing with the unknown – the easier it gets. It certainly works for public speaking.

For those who feel travelling is dangerous, consider this: if you are comfortable going into a city such as Toronto, New York, Paris, Los Angeles, San Francisco, Washington, etc., realize there could be as much danger there as in most emerging or developing countries you'll visit. When travelling, do your homework and take basic precautions: travel in groups or with another person, not alone; carry a photocopy of your passport with you, not the original; and carry a light fabric wallet on a strap that hangs around your neck or wraps around your waist. Stop worrying about theft; just enjoy your visit.

We can't imagine life without travelling. We fall in love with each other all over again wherever we go. When we talk to locals in other countries, they sometimes say things like, "I don't blame you for coming here. I heard about the shootings in Toronto; it isn't safe in your country. And your trains – they're not safe, they blow up and there are no regulations. I wouldn't go to NY either," they add. "I saw those buildings being attacked." We are always amazed at the different perceptions abroad: while other countries may appear unsafe to us, people living in those countries sometimes have that same

Chapter 1

exaggerated perception of our country. Unexpected misfortunes can come about in your own country. Of course, some countries experience civil and political crises and tourists should avoid those areas, but there is so much to discover. Fear should not discourage anyone from travelling.

Learn to face your fear and step out of your comfort zone. Once you accomplish this, you will grow as a person and you will prosper. Pushing your limits will open new avenues through which you can be successful and reach your goals. Do you think most people are comfortable going into business? Of course there is some fear, but one must overcome that and persevere. Don't let fear ruin your chance of reaching your goals.

Often we sabotage our own successes because we fear failure (that fear also appears on lists of top fears). For many it remains a somewhat unconscious scapegoat, the reason they avoid investing effort in achieving a goal.

There are so many opportunities in life. Seize them. Don't miss out. Live with no regrets. The most successful people in the world *do* experience fear. The difference is that they understand it and don't allow it to immobilize them. Understand that most successful entrepreneurs have failed more times than they can count on one hand. The difference is that they have learned from their mistakes and are persistent in achieving success. Of course, although failure to some may simply be a learning experience, for most of us it is a traumatic experience that sticks in our throat and grabs the nervous system. Failure is different for everyone; each person associates a different level of pain with failure. It is up to you to link fear to learning, as difficult as that may seem.

We failed at many things before finding the right balance and finally achieving the success we desired: we both failed with our first marriages, we failed with some investments and we failed to choose the right tenants. But with all these failures came life lessons and valuable experience. Don't allow fear to stop you from achieving the goals and dreams you want – strive to reach them. Perseverance:

that's the challenge in life.

Maybe a teacher once told you that you would amount to nothing; perhaps your family has not been supportive. You might have been humiliated at some point and you didn't like yourself. Maybe you're still struggling to rebuild your self-esteem. If you have these feelings about yourself or if you've had traumatic experiences, don't let them damage your chance to succeed. Learn not to carry these negative neuro-associations – either use them to motivate yourself or learn to drop them altogether. Often, bad past experiences can lower our self-esteem and destroy our true potential.

Learn from your mistakes and don't repeat them. Assess your failures and address any element that you can improve immediately by including some mini "action plans" in your to-do list. Maybe your mistake has taught you that you took on more than you could handle. Perhaps you learned that you could have asked for help and that missing a deadline can be very costly. Perhaps you now realize that you don't have the answers to everything and seeking expertise is warranted. But know that you have the power to transform yourself. Spend time with positive people and those who are successful and brilliant. Expand your social network to include people who have common goals and learn from them as they will learn from you. Never second guess whether you have what it takes or whether you are talented or competent enough.

If the majority of your thoughts are negative, you will definitely be limiting your potential for success, and fear will be ever-present. But if you surround yourself with positive people and spend your days in positive, productive settings, your thoughts will more likely be positive ones. You will gain confidence as you realize that some of these positive people have succeeded with perhaps more fear, less knowledge and less talent than you have. By moving in these spheres and connecting with these fortunate few, your relationship with the fear of failure will change.

Remember that all successful people feel and experience fear at one time or another. You are not the only one to have these negative

Chapter 1

feelings. Fear is necessary to make us use caution in our actions and decisions. Use caution to your advantage and use not-so-positive feelings to motivate yourself and challenge your limitations.

We believe one of the best motivational speakers is Zig Ziglar, also the author of 14 books. The following paragraph, from Zig's July 14, 2009 *Newsletter*, describes how you can flush out some of the fear you may be experiencing:

> How do we overcome fear? First we must learn to examine our fears. Example: Giving a speech...If that's your fear, ask yourself a few questions. "Why am I afraid to make a speech? Is it because I'm afraid of being rejected? Then why do I think I'll be rejected? Do I believe what I'm about to say? Is my speech worth giving? Am I proud of the comments I'm about to make?" As you ask yourself these questions, the fear will begin to subside. It subsides because you have explored your subconscious mind with your questions and flushed out some of your fears.

A Few Fortunate Thoughts about the Way You Think

- Understand how you associate pain or pleasure with different tasks and how this will determine the drive and effort needed to accomplish your goals. Learn to associate pleasure with those tasks that might appear challenging by focusing on the end result: financial freedom.

- Reflect on where you are in life and where you want to be; assess what is holding you back from achieving your goals. Is it bad habits like procrastination? Is it fear of failure, humiliation or being judged? Turn these negatives into positives by developing your awareness and taking action. Taking ownership and control of your life is empowering.

- Determine who your positive influences are. Drop negative influences in your life. Meet with people who are successful or who have attained the goals you want to reach. Gain their insight and knowledge.

- Assess your drive: do you want more out of life or are you content? Only you can answer this question. If you are content and happy with what you have accomplished, you are already among the fortunate few. If you want more out of life then go for it! Nothing stops you from achieving your goals. You control your thinking; no one else does. Think positive, take action and you will achieve all you desire.

Chapter 2
Assessing Your Relationship with Money

Money won't create success, the freedom to make it will.

Nelson Mandela

Beautiful British Columbia

Carole

British Columbia is a wonderful place, especially in the springtime. We decided to spend a week on the West Coast to visit old friends and get an early start on summer – Vancouver's microclimate means thousands of cherry trees start blooming in February. This incredible city is like a large pink flowerbed with the majestic white peaks of the Coast Mountains on one side and the dark blue waters of the Pacific Ocean on the other. I lived in BC for 10 years and I'm still completely in awe each time I visit. As soon as I step off the plane, I can smell the fresh air coming from the mountains and over the ocean and it is pure delight.

Daniel and I headed straight to Stanley Park as soon as we landed. We laced up our hiking shoes and set out to walk the whole seawall, an 8.8 kilometre pedestrian walkway hugging the park's shoreline. Daniel had his camera and zoomed off ahead of me – he had just spotted the collection of colourful totem poles at the entrance of the park. He was fascinated by the carving of the creatures' eyes – the whale, the wolf, the frog and especially the eagle, his favourite animal, representing the kingdom of the air in the Haida culture. Part of the poles' romance is that they do not last – the coastal elements eat away at the cedar over time.

Back on the path, Daniel stopped many times to take pictures as every turn offered a scenic view. We decided to enter the park to get closer to the trees. Tall and majestic, there stood cedar, hemlock and fir trees – the smell of moss, damp leaves and pine drew us deeper into the forest. We stumbled on what has to be the most gigantic of all trees: the Hollow Tree, a 700- to 800-year-old Western Red Cedar stump and one of the best-known and most-photographed landmarks in the park. I remember seeing historic photographs showing cars, and even an elephant, posing inside the tree's large cavity. Daniel did not miss his chance to snap more pictures of this imposing conifer.

We were getting cold, so we decided to find a café, where we enjoyed a nice warm hot chocolate with whipped cream. Daniel showed me all the pictures he had taken – it was our first day in Vancouver and already we were overwhelmed by the beauty of our surroundings. It was wonderful to reconnect with nature and the friends we visited during our stay and to experience such wonders in our homeland. Canada is a beautiful country!

Chapter 2

Stanley Park, Vancouver, Canada.

Our experience at Stanley Park involved no cost. There is much to see and experience around us without spending money. Seeing the white-capped mountains, the giant trees, the lush gardens cost nothing. Snapping those pictures – priceless. Defining your needs and wants is your choice. If you are able to order a $300 bottle of wine for dinner, go for it! But realize that you can experience much for little. The giant trees stop growing after reaching a certain height. Once you have grown your wealth to a certain level, you too can stop and choose to now enjoy what life has to offer. You're in control.

Chapter 2

How Much Money Do You Really Need?

We'd like to begin talking about money by saying that we believe financial literacy is missing from our education system and it is important to educate oneself in this important subject. Most of us can't make a connection between the state of our country's economy and the way we manage our own finances, let alone set a long-term budget. The principle of good household finance practice applies to this country's economy and it's important we understand how money flows in and out of Canada. Raising the level of knowledge and improving our personal finances will positively affect the status of our country's economy, just as bad personal debt has a negative impact on our economy. We trust that one day our education system will make personal finances an important part of the curriculum.

There are professional financial planners, but few of them can present a global approach to finances. Some are very knowledgeable; however, most tend to stick to their niche or specialty. We are not trying to discredit the financial planning profession but are simply saying "beware." We have discovered that some financial planners are trained mainly to sell products in which the company they work for has a vested interest – profits. So you really must understand your own finances.

How much money do you need to be financially independent? A financial plan and budget will help you determine your road map to fulfilling your objectives. This plan will guide your steps toward your goals, but the amount of money you need depends on the lifestyle and standard of living you want and the elements you consider key to your quality of life. What are your expectations?

One day, we were sitting in a café in Costa Rica next to a man who seemed to be a local. He asked us where we were from. We answered, "Toronto, Canada – but now, we spend the winter here, in this beautiful country, and sometimes in other countries with warm weather." We introduced ourselves and asked his name.

"My name is Rodríguez." We continued our conversation by asking what his occupation was.

"I am a business man," he replied. We asked what kind of business he was in. "I raise cattle." We were interested to learn more about his business since Guanacaste, the province where we live, is known as the cattle and ranch region of Costa Rica. We continued chatting and asked how large his farm was. To our surprise, he told us he owned six cows. We asked him if his business provided enough for him to live on. He answered with a wide smile, "Yes, I feed my family and have enough to trade for other things such as bread, vegetables, clothing, books, cellphone, TV and all we need." He then added, "As a matter of fact, I just finished work."

"Finished work?" we exclaimed. "But it's nine in the morning!"

He explained. "Yes. I start at 7:30 and do what I have to do and finish at 8:30 AM."

We laughed and said, "You worked one hour."

He said, "Yes," looking at us with a puzzled expression. We asked him about his plans for the rest of the day. He said, "Well, I am going to do what I do almost every day. I will head back home, wash up, then take my wife to her sister's. There, we play cards. Afterwards, I'll probably play my guitar with a friend at his restaurant, and then have lunch because the restaurant provides me free lunch for free entertainment. Then, I will pick up my wife at her sister's and have a little siesta with her until around 2 PM. Afterwards, I'll walk to school and meet up with the kids and take them to the beach to play with them. The kids love it!"

We wanted to know more about his business and continued with our questions: "So have you ever considered getting more cattle and perhaps selling exotic organic beef to North America or abroad? You might have a product that you can offer that no other farmers do. We have noticed that your cattle are very different here, with their long, rabbit-like ears."

He asked, "Why would I do that?"

We wanted to explain how he could grow his business. "Well, you

Chapter 2

could probably contract with supermarket chains in the United States and Canada and eventually make millions!"

He quickly retorted, "What would that bring me?"

We continued with our explanation: "Well, you could have a million-dollar farming operation – tractors, big barns, many staff and a slaughterhouse."

"OK," he paused, "and I would have to put a lot of hours and work into that. What about my family?"

"They would be rich and you could provide them with so much more."

To our surprise, he interrupted and said, "But I already provide for them, and unlike you Americans, I spend lots of time with my family. I work very few hours. I love spending time with my wife and every day is like a holiday here in what you people call paradise. With your plan, when would I play guitar with my best friend, which I love doing, and how could I ever spend that precious time with my wife every day if I had to work long hours? And what about my kids? Who would walk them home from school and play with them?" He lowered his head, a distressed look on his face.

We looked at each other and then turned to him. "You're right, don't change anything." He looked at us with his brown eyes as we concluded, "Actually, you are the one doing everything right. Many of us are doing things wrong; it's a matter of choice and it is obvious yours is the best one for you." We felt we had more explaining to do, and continued, "Rodríguez, many Americans strive for the life you have but it's only after retirement or getting rich that most can have the kind of life you live. You are living a dream, a life many envy. Our culture is very different from yours; we have much to learn from you. Thank you!" His eyes opened wide and he looked very pleased. As we shook hands, he pulled us in and gave us a hug.

If what you want is a life that lets you sleep in, have breakfast and read, play squash, have lunch, do a little office work, siesta with your spouse, go kayaking, have dinner, and meet friends by the ocean for a glass of wine at sunset, then you have to figure out how much money you need and have a clear understanding of what financial freedom means *to you*.

We have decided to live a life of freedom. Simply put, we live our dream. Like Rodríguez, we are among the fortunate few and you can be too. We are financially free and we feel very fortunate to spend our days as we want and to be free to undertake projects such as writing this book. We decide when and what we want to do. We live in the best country ever, with no one dictating, by and large, what we can and cannot do. Like Rodríguez, who is living the lifestyle he has chosen within his means, we are free to make our own decisions and live life as we choose within our own budget. Your budget depends on your expectations in life. If you want to spend more time with your children, your family or your friends or to be involved in your community, this has to be part of your plan. If you want a yacht, you need to include this goal in your plan too.

We're going to talk more about budgeting later. For now, suffice it to say that you must make your budget simple enough that it works for you. Your budget is your guideline and should not take over your life; don't start counting your pennies and don't become obsessed with money. Simply stay on track and live within your means. Manage your life like a business and you will always be ahead of the game. Don't go crazy if your partner goes for an expensive fancy coffee or buys an extra pair of shoes one day. Monitor your total spending together every month, make sure you stay on budget and celebrate your progress paying off any debts.

What Is Financial Independence?

What does financial independence really mean? Many financial experts use the term and the definition varies from person to person. For some, financial independence means balancing your budget (revenues and expenses) and having no debt. For many people it means not having to worry about money, being able to live comfortably and having a source of income that fits their lifestyle without them having to hold a job. For others, it means having enough money to chase a dream and simply being able to do what they always wanted to do.

When we ask people what they consider financial independence, they often say, "If I was making the same amount of money as I'm making now without working, that would be financial independence." The definition of financial independence can adapt to every individual. We define financial independence as having sufficient personal wealth or income to have the quality of life you want, without having to actively work to cover your expenses. Generally speaking, financially independent people rely on assets that generate income that is greater than their expenses.

Financial independence also means you have the freedom, options and means to pursue your grandest goals: working on your own projects on your own terms, creating art, taking dance lessons, hiking, canoeing, taking guitar lessons, doing yoga, travelling – whatever you've always wanted to do.

It doesn't matter how old or young someone is or how much money they have or make. If they can generate enough money to meet their needs from sources other than a primary occupation, they have achieved financial independence. If they are 25 years old and their expenses are $3,000 per month and they have assets that generate $3,001 per month, they have achieved financial independence and they have the freedom to enjoy things those who hold regular jobs don't have. On the other hand, someone could be 50 years old and earn $100,000 a month but have monthly expenses beyond $100,000, therefore not qualifying as financially independent.

If you are an average-earning Canadian or American, understand that you are already wealthier than the vast majority of people on Earth and are among the most fortunate: the median after-tax income for Canadian families in which the person with the highest income was younger than 65 was $73,300 in 2011, while for senior households it was $49,300. Most North Americans have never known the true meaning of poverty. This is not to say that poverty does not exist in our own backyards; we know it does. The notion of being rich changes dramatically depending on your perspective and North Americans in general are wealthy compared with most people in most emerging countries.

Statistics indicate that the average Canadian earns a decent salary. So why is it that many do not achieve financial independence? How is it that a doctor earning $200,000 or $300,000 a year may end up with less in the bank than someone making $40,000 a year? You will find answers to these questions in later chapters. It is all based on planning, perseverance and hard work. It is about knowing yourself and differentiating between your needs and your wants.

The point we want to make is that determining how much money you need to live the life you want determines what financial independence is for you.

Most retirees we know are in a position of financial independence, most living the lifestyle they had while they were working while now collecting a single pension. Many planned to – and do – live very comfortably. According to Statistics Canada in *A Portrait of Seniors in Canada* (2006 update),

> [S]eniors have more positive assessments of their finances than individuals in younger age groups… Among individuals aged 65 to 74 with total household incomes of less than $30,000, the average level of financial satisfaction was 6.1 [out of 10], compared with a score of 5.1 among individuals aged 25 to 54. The same pattern is evident within higher income categories.

Let's be clear about debt. Some people will say that financial independence means having no debt. However, we have debt and we consider ourselves financially independent. We own a few homes that still have mortgages and we borrow against our line of credit to invest. (This is called leveraging. We also use a technique called the Smith Manoeuvre; we'll cover it in Chapter 6, Equity Is Power.) This type of debt can be termed good debt because it helps us earn our living. Financial independence for us means we have sufficient income to cover all payments – including debt payments – and live our desired lifestyle, even with debt.

Whatever your situation, it all comes down to having enough to maintain your lifestyle without having to go to work every day. We know that for many, being mortgage-free is part of being financially independent. In most cases, we agree. Your principal home should bear no mortgage before you call yourself financially independent.

Another important point is this: the era of working for a single employer your whole career is long gone and with it, reliable and generous benefit and pension plans. The demographic forecasts in Canada, with its aging population and the 2008 financial crisis, with its market volatility and uncertainty, have blurred the financial horizon for many people. Taking your finances seriously and looking after your own future are critical to achieving financial independence.

This brings us to an important part of attaining financial freedom: planning. We'll discuss planning and go into detail about the importance of to-do lists in Chapter 3, where we'll show you a Life Planning Worksheet. This worksheet will have you list your wants and desires – they will become your goals. For now, start by thinking about these questions:

- Do I want to make changes to my life?
- Do I want to change jobs or would I like a promotion?
- Do I want a family or a life mate?
- Do I want freedom to travel and do as I want without the fear of running out of money?

We will come back to these important questions later, but answering them honestly will help you to define and achieve your goals.

What are the steps required in achieving financial independence? However you define financial independence, you will find yourself taking advice from articles or speakers that relate to you and your goals. You are responsible for you own education: read widely, watch television programs, search the web, go to conferences and talk to people around you who have found the motivation to bring change, growth and wealth in their lives.

How Has Debt Changed?

Our grandparents did not buy anything unless they had cash on hand to purchase it. Now we purchase furniture, cars, boats, appliances – anything – on the "have it now, pay later" model. We call this buying on credit. How convenient! But there is a cost to that instant convenience and it is called interest.

Retailers and banks have mastered the technique of instilling in people the need to have what they want now and pay for it later so that these companies can collect interest. They have also learned to make us believe our wants are actually needs and have become huge profit-makers in the process. They use neuro-associative conditioning and subliminal marketing techniques to manipulate our emotions and influence us to buy even when we don't have the money on hand.

If you understand how neuro-association works, you can begin to make better choices by associating the right emotions with your decisions. Companies got smart by playing to our weaknesses, making us experience instant gratification by "having it now." To counter this marketing powerhouse, you need to learn to associate paying interest with pain. Doing so can help you make better decisions about buying on credit.

The buy-now, pay-later philosophy was one of the major causes of the US's 2008 economic downfall and of the vulnerable situation of everyone who owns a credit card. Debt is also a major cause of divorce and family breakdown. Marriages often fail because out-of-control finances create stress and generate a lot of tension.

Chapter 2

Mortgage Insurance:
Personal Pain for the Greater Good

One reason Canadians were not in quite as bad a position as our neighbours in the US at the time of the financial crash in 2008 is the existence of such guardrails as the insurance that the Canadian Mortgage and Housing Corporation (CMHC) imposes on some people purchasing homes. We were also fortunate that our Canadian banking system quickly reacted to the 1998 economic crisis, setting new mortgage regulations to avoid accumulation of extensive debt. Some of these measures might make it difficult for first-time home buyers to qualify for a mortgage but they safeguard our economy as a whole.

Mortgage default insurance, commonly referred to as CMHC insurance, is mandatory in Canada for home purchases with down payments between 5% (the minimum required in Canada) and 19.99%. Mortgage default insurance protects lenders if a homeowner defaults on their mortgage. In our concrete world, when the homeowner fails to pay their mortgage they are forced into foreclosure. This means the bank takes over their house and makes a claim to the CMHC for any money they may have lost on the deal. CMHC then returns that money to the bank to cover the loss. In Canada, the bank insures its mortgage loan by having the homeowner pay for the coverage.

Although mortgage default insurance costs homebuyers between 1.80% and 3.15% of their mortgage amount, it is actually beneficial to the buyer market. Without it, mortgage rates would be higher because the risk of default would increase. Lenders are able to offer lower mortgage rates when mortgages are protected by default insurance because the risk of default is spread across multiple home buyers.

When we first purchased a home and had to pay for CMHC insurance, it frustrated us, but once we understood the reason for it, we came to appreciate it.

Bad Debt vs. Good Debt

Bad debt

A 2013 survey by Abacus Data found that 70% of Canadians pay their credit card balance off in full every month. Thirty percent do not pay off their total, instead paying large interest charges.

According to the Canadian Bankers Association, credit cards account for just 5.5% of total household debt. Canadians use their credit cards wisely compared with our American neighbours. There has been improvement among US consumers since the recession hit in 2008 but the proportions are the reverse of what they are in Canada. In 2013, only 28.7% of credit card accounts were paid off in full each month in the US. And that's a 50% increase since early 2008, when just 19% of Americans paid off their cards in full each month. The interest rates credit card companies charge make any credit card debt bad debt.

Here's an example of just how negative bad debt can be: A student graduates from university and secures a decent-paying job. He has a six-month interest-free period to pay off his $20,000 student loan. He is unable to pay it off in six months so he puts the loan on two credit cards.

Most Canadian credit cards have interest rates ranging between 17% and 21%, so let's pick 19% for this scenario. Our student decides to make just the minimum payment on his cards so that he can continue living the lifestyle he chooses. After all, he thinks, it's only $20,000; someday soon he will be earning a six-figure income. He brushes the debt off, figuring he can always deal with it later.

Our former student continues paying the minimum required on his card for 20 years – it seemed like other expenses were always coming up. But one day, he realizes where he's at with his finances. His $20,000 student loan has now cost him $76,720. It was so easy to make the minimum payment that he never thought about the consequences of not paying the principal balance.

Chapter 2

Don't ever think you can just coast and pay the minimum. This is bad debt, very bad debt.

Daniel learned a very important lesson about debt payment at age 17 when his father sold him his car and helped him get a loan from the bank. Daniel made the monthly payments for a year until one day, he had saved a few thousand dollars. He thought perhaps he should pay off the car loan; after all, the remaining amount would be easy to cover since he had made payments every month. To his surprise, the loan was almost the same size it had been a year before. He had paid mostly interest and very little on the loan amount itself. He was furious, but came to realize the importance of making payments well beyond the amount requested by the lender. This is something you must absolutely teach your children as Daniel's father taught him.

Bad debt often arises when you over-spend and consume material goods beyond your means, buying on credit and not being able to pay the full balance at the end of the month. Doing that is really just buying things you can't afford and it's unhealthy. Uncontrolled credit card debt is often a precursor to a serious personal financial crisis.

Our advice against buying what you can't afford extends to using your credit cards to purchase vacations. Unless you're paying off your card in full each month, this is bad debt. We understand that the thought of a vacation is wonderful, but if it doesn't fit your budget, don't do it. Stay disciplined and save for it instead.

Bad debt can also arise when you invest without doing your homework. Remember, if something sounds too good to be true, it most likely is. We invested in a hotel in Aylmer, Quebec, and this proved to be a bad debt. But we learned an important lesson from it. Do your homework and make sure you know exactly what you are investing in and with whom you are doing business. Understanding your investments reduces the level of risk and reduces the chance of it turning into bad debt.

Good debt

Being smart about your purchases is obviously the right thing to do. Most of us know in our hearts when we've made a wrong decision. Control your impulses and stick to your budget. This is your future you're dealing with and you don't want to be in a situation where you are left with bad debt and aren't able to get out of it.

Debt comes in many forms. You might borrow for a mortgage, you might borrow to invest in your registered retirement savings plan (called leveraging) or you might have a student loan. Taking a student loan, for example, may serve you well because you are investing in yourself, increasing your earning potential. That's good debt (as long as you pay it off!). Taking money from your line of credit to make an investment that will earn you more than the interest you pay on your credit line is another example of good debt – it increases your earnings.

Turning bad debt into good

Daniel

I have an interesting story about turning bad debt into good debt. In the 1980s, when I was 19 and my business partner, whom we'll call Richard, was 17, we were fearless and hungry for success. We had started a little business called We Do It All. The local newspaper heard about two teens starting a business instead of working for someone else during the summer holidays and did a front-page article on us, which helped make our business successful. Soon we changed the business name to Quality Decks and Driveways and in time had seven employees. This success motivated Richard to purchase his first property while he was still in high school.

Richard was just a teenager but was very mature and ahead of his time. He was sharp and quick and knew how to make things work to his advantage – including credit cards. At that time many credit cards were issued interest-free for the first six months. It was an aggressive promotion in a highly competitive market designed to entice customers to choose a particular card, to switch providers or – even better – to add another card to their collection. No financial institution would lend a 17-year-old money, let alone give him a mortgage. Richard had my father co-sign so that he could get his own mortgage of $69,000. This allowed him to purchase his own principal home, a small townhouse. He rented rooms to college students while living there himself to help with mortgage payments.

Soon after, Richard and I bought another property as an investment and took advantage of one of the "interest-free for six months" credit cards. Since banks would not lend us money without 5% down, we both applied for credit cards and used them toward our down payment on that property. The end of the sixth month came soon enough and we had to start paying interest. Richard came up with a wonderful idea: he suggested we apply for another credit card from a different financial institution offering the same no interest for six months deal. We did exactly that and paid off the original debt and cancelled our first cards. This scheme allowed us to purchase a home with a 5% down payment at no expense or interest to us for one year. We've used similar techniques over the years. That second house was rented to students. With the surplus in rental income and personal savings, we managed to pay off the second card, which carried the down payment.

Choose your credit wisely

Using your credit card intelligently should be part of your success strategy. Credit cards allow you more buying power without paying any interest (if you pay in full and on time!) and they also help you establish a great credit rating.

Beware of the department store card scammers, however. They are like predators; they will lure you in with all techniques available to them: zero down payment, no interest for a year, 15% reduction on your purchase. But once you register for the card, you are trapped in the credit scammer's web. You will realize after you sign on the dotted line that there is $45 administration fee. Then you will find out there is a hidden yearly membership fee or you may discover that the item you purchased at no interest for a year is on sale at a competitor for 50% off. Don't be swayed by their sneaky manoeuvres. With your regular credit card you can purchase any of these department store items, without adding another card to your collection. Just make sure you can pay off the balance by the end of the month, and take advantage of any Air Miles or other points system your card offers. We have taken numerous trips using our Air Miles; it's a great way to fit a trip into a small budget. If the trip still doesn't fit, it isn't the right time for it. Wait until you can afford it and be aware that you are making a good business decision.

For more on good debt and bad debt we recommend the book *Rich Dad, Poor Dad* by Robert Kiyosaki. It advocates financial independence and building wealth through investing (including real estate investing), starting and owning businesses and increasing one's financial intelligence.

A Few Fortunate Thoughts about Your Relationship with Money

- Realize that how much money you need depends on your aspirations in life. Being among the fortunate few does not mean you need to be filthy rich. It only means having the lifestyle you wish for without working the traditional 35-hour week.
- Live within your means. Only you can control this. Get rid of the buy-now, pay-later model. Understand your buying habits – this is key to healthy budgeting.
- Understand good debt and bad debt so you can make educated decisions. Scrutinize all debt you take on – it must lead to a positive outcome, such as a sound real estate investment. Eliminating bad debt should be part of your plan.

Chapter 3
Time Management and Planning

A goal without a plan is just a wish.

Antoine de Saint-Exupéry

Lost in time, Maui, Hawaii

We travelled to Hawaii for two weeks just before Christmas. Hawaii is magical and simply one the most romantic places in the world. For those reasons, we invited Daniel's parents to join us on that trip to mark their 40th wedding anniversary.

This beautiful island attracts true nature lovers and people seeking tranquility. Maui has a number of quaint towns and artist communities and has retained that remote, small-community feel. We felt right at home. We found our favourite location for breakfast, went dining and dancing and took numerous walks along the beach as the sun set. We took the scenic road to Hana, the undisputed number one attraction on the island. We saw countless waterfalls along the way, with lush, green tropical forests and black sand beaches. We also discovered a great snorkelling reef just off Molokini Island. The boat ride there was breathtaking and curious sea turtles came to great us. Our snorkelling adventure was spectacular, but we must admit we got a little nervous when we saw a shark slowly swim a few metres below us. It is a whole new world to discover beneath the sea.

Such beauty and the relaxed atmosphere can really turn off your inner clock – in fact, we were so out of touch with reality that we showed up one day late for departure at the airport! Can you imagine how silly we felt? Four adults! We could not believe it when the check-in attendant asked us bluntly, "Do you know what day it is?" We all looked at each other and nervously grabbed our phones, which had remained at the bottom of our bags most of the trip. You should have seen our faces. We were supposed to fly out on the 24th…but drove ourselves to the airport with our luggage on the 25th. None of us had a clue we were a day late.

Noting our surprise and dismay, the attendant quickly started punching numbers on her computer without asking a single question. Minutes later she turned to us and said with the warmest smile, "Please leave your luggage with me and run to gate 12 – the next flight to Toronto leaves in 25 minutes. Mele kalikimaka" – Merry Christmas!

Chapter 3

Romance in Maui, USA.

Time Management and Planning

Every time we hear something about Hawaii, it takes us back to the time we were 24 hours late for our flight and it's a reminder that the one thing we do own is time – and we must use it wisely. How frequently does time escape us and how often do we run out of time for a given task? As you get older, you understand that time is precious. Planning is key when you want to reach a goal, and there are tools and good habits you can integrate into your life to get there efficiently.

Chapter 3

Stop Wasting Time and Brain Power

It is easy to sabotage your own destiny and goals by wasting time and brain power.

Wasting time includes such activities as social networking – that means spending time on Facebook, Twitter, Google+, Tumblr, etc. – unless of course it is to promote your business. Wasting time also includes spending hours on the phone gossiping, endlessly shopping, watching "just one more" YouTube video and playing three hours of Internet golf every day. Perhaps your time-waster is a bad habit you got into years ago or a daily routine that's not productive, such as watching too much TV or endlessly playing Candy Crush. Are you the type of person who gets caught up in chatting? Perhaps you see someone in the hallway at work and the next thing you know you've been talking for 40 minutes instead of working. Maybe that chat included some complaining about work overload and long hours...

These habits can delay your success and prevent you from reaching your goals. Make a conscious decision to gain control over your own agenda and change your habits and daily routine if necessary. There is always room for improvement.

Wasting brain power can be avoided by simply delegating or automating processes. Sometimes we fall into patterns and complete tasks mechanically, although inefficiently, without paying attention to the process. Take a hard look at what you do every day, especially the things that consume lots of time and come up regularly on your work schedule. When Daniel worked in IT, he used to input information into an exchange server each time a person changed job titles or a new person was hired in the organization. Finally, Daniel spoke with his employer and the process was automated by creating a link with the human resources department's database. Sometimes looking at what consumes brain power can help us streamline processes, diminish the risk of errors and become more effective.

Another element that can't be ignored when talking about time management is outsourcing. Outsourcing can be a valuable tool to help you get things done or to manage your affairs while you are busy accomplishing something else. Consider outsourcing if you are overwhelmed or if the task is outside your expertise. You can easily hire people to do such tasks as bookkeeping or managing your website, saving you hours and days of work.

Note that this type of outsourcing is different from having experts such as lawyers and mortgage brokers as part of your team, which we'll talk about in Chapter 4. Members of your team need to understand your long-term goals and be aware of your overall plans – there needs to be a shared vision and the accomplishment of their tasks and the incorporation of their advice must converge on the realization of your goals. The kind of outsourcing we're referring to now involves hiring people who will usually concentrate on the task you assign to them and will limit their contributions to that specific element without getting involved in your greater goals or vision.

To-Do Lists

One of the foundations of success is the to-do list. The alert reader will have noticed that we have mentioned them several times. You might be thinking, "What?" But it's true.

Many of us relate success to multitasking, but when you have a lot on the go, it is difficult to remember everything you need to do on a given day. A daily to-do list will help keep you on track – just a glance at your list takes you straight to whatever it is you need to focus on. Humans have a hard time remembering more than seven items at a time – we can hold onto about seven pieces of information for just 20 to 30 *seconds* in short-term memory.

We have always relied on to-do lists and are still using them in the early retirement stage of our lives to bring structure to our days and to remain productive. Putting together a daily to-do list will help you remember an appointment, prepare for a meeting or follow up with a business matter. Having a to-do list will improve your organizational skills. It helps you manage your life and gets you one step closer to your goals. A list brings clarity to your vision as you strive to reach each of your goals. It also helps manage your and your partner's responsibilities: sharing, delegating and taking care of "who does what." You can keep track of your accomplishments; tasks you were not able to complete are simply moved to the next day. Before you know it, everything you added to your to-do list has been done, new items have been added and the cycle has taken you from one day to the next.

A to-do list keeps you focused; as you cross off completed tasks you feel a sense of progress, accomplishment and satisfaction. This sense of accomplishment will motivate you and keep the momentum going. You will come to realize that even in this busy life of yours you can get things done. When you have 20 items on your to-do list and you notice by noon you have crossed off half, you'll know you've achieved some of your personal objectives. This in turn affirms your progress and motivates you to complete the list. Without the list you wouldn't realize what you had accomplished, you would simply continue to feel overwhelmed. Seeing items crossed off gives you the drive to do more.

Later in this chapter when we discuss planning – that is, writing down what it is you want to achieve in your life – you will understand that the to-do list will help you get there faster and with less stress. For example, if your plan is to own three houses within five years, the items you put on your list are the steps you need to take on that particular day to take you closer to that goal, perhaps contacting your mortgage broker, getting legal advice on owning more than one house and studying the market. If your goal is to learn Spanish within five years, you have to define the steps on your to-do list. Without the plan and without the list, five years will pass you by – *el tiempo vuela* – but you still won't be able to speak Spanish and you will still own only one home.

You may still be asking yourself why you need to use a to-do list. Think about it: your life is busy; you have a million things on your plate. After working all day you have to take little Jimmy to hockey practice and little Sara to karate. You have to get your income taxes filed. You have to go online to pay your Visa bill before it's due. You need to finish painting after that renovation project, get the kids' lunches ready for tomorrow and do a load of laundry and on and on and on. How are you ever going to get all this done? And on top of it, you have decided you want to focus on your goals.

With all your day-to-day tasks, it is easy to become overwhelmed and easy to get discouraged – and to forget things and ignore things. We felt this way at times, but thanks to our to-do lists, we stayed on course. We had a son to raise, five properties to manage, eight tenants to deal with, several websites to manage, investment portfolios to manage and, before we gave them up, our full-time jobs. Friends would ask how we juggled it all. The answer is organization, and our to-do lists do exactly that. It is easy to put things on hold when you have a million things on the go. Having everything you need to accomplish written down in list format makes things tangible and manageable. It clarifies what tasks need to be tackled first and it does not allow you to forget or put things off. It therefore helps you manage and accomplish all you set out to do, if not today, then surely tomorrow. Every day you will have a new to-do list and you will never feel overwhelmed again.

Another thing we like about our to-do lists is that when we sit down every morning to write our list for the day, it opens up important discussions and allows us to share our ideas and talk about our plans.

In today's world we have so many distractions. You might say, "I will check my Facebook account for five minutes." But then two hours just pass you by. It's not just the Internet. There's family, friends, community commitments and the list goes on. If you use to-do lists you will find yourself making the items on the list your priority. Your list helps you prioritize tasks and forces you to be a time management expert; it encourages you to stay focused, keeping your attention on what is important.

When you are organized and invest energy in reaching a goal, you often exceed the goals set in your plan. For example, we had a goal of owning five properties within five years, but we achieved it in three. This gave us a sense of accomplishment and it motivated us. We succeeded thanks to our Life Planning Worksheet, but mostly thanks to our to-do lists.

Write out a to-do list every day. You can sit in bed with your partner in the evening and, while reviewing your day, start writing out those things you want on your to-do list for tomorrow. We usually do our to-do list every morning. It is important for us to agree on our list, and sharing these tasks is a form of multitasking for a couple. Having a sense of ownership keeps us both on the path toward the realization of our goals.

You will improve at creating to-do lists and with time, you will also get better at accomplishing all the tasks on that list. There were times we had so many items on a list that we looked at each other like two deer in the headlights. But by the end of the day, we were surprised and satisfied to discover that we had accomplished everything. We became so efficient, it was like an art. You will develop tricks and techniques for getting things done. For example, we did all our follow-ups and phone calls early in the morning and at the end of the day on our way to and from work, when we still had jobs. Those of you who drive in and out of metropolitan areas will want to make the most of Bluetooth technology and those otherwise wasted hours on the road. If you have lunch at your desk, you have at your disposal all the tools to accomplish a major part of your to-do list. If your employer micromanages and you are not able to do personal task on work computers or phones during your breaks, use your smartphone.

Are you busy, or productive?

For the past 10 years, to-do lists have been our plans for the day and have determined whether we would be productive or not. For some, being productive means doing more and for others, it means doing less. Let's not confuse being busy with productivity. Being productive means doing things that bring you closer to your goals. How can you be productive without adding stress? Being busy is stressful; being productive is not because it means you are accomplishing things, thus eliminating stress. You want to be productive but also make it a pleasurable experience. Being realistic will help you enjoy success and avoid disappointment.

Our definition of "productivity" is accomplishing the items we put on our to-do list. We stay focused and have a clear understanding of what needs to be done to bring us toward our goals. Although being productive means different things to different people, it invariably generates a feeling of control and satisfaction. Take the time to analyze what being productive means to you, what your needs and expectations are for leisure, work, personal business, etc., and make sure there's balance in your life. Pinpoint the things that take up too much of your time during your normal daily routine and replace them with tasks that make you more productive. Challenge yourself in this exercise. What rhythm suits you – are you more productive in the morning or at night? Once you have determined what set of activities you need to perform to steady your evolution toward your own success, you will have mastered your own definition of productivity.

One final note: you may at first think making lists will be tedious, but you'll actually enjoy doing your to-do lists once you get started because they will give you a sense of satisfaction every day. For more information and examples of to-do lists go to *TheFortunateFew.com.* Start writing your to-do list today!

Put Your Life on Autopilot – Automate or Delegate!

Automation

One day we were doing our to-do lists long distance because one of us was out of town. These are the results:

Daniel

- Prepare & rehearse lecture
- Go to meeting at 1 PM
- Network Security meeting at 2 PM

Chapter 3

- Deposit tenants' post-dated cheques
- Look over legal documents
- Ask IT-in-Mind to make change on website and blog
- Proof read and edit
- Look for editor and publisher for book
- Answer online discussions
- Go to cleaners

Carole

- Proof read minister's speech
- Make appointment for photo shoot
- Pay cable, Internet and phone bills online
- Make dentist appointment for Corey
- Pay MasterCard bill
- Send out press release
- Phone parents
- Book a flight to Ottawa for conference
- Get birthday gift for sister
- Go to gym
- Figure out how to **manage our time more efficiently**

All of that to do, and at the end, figure out **how to manage our time more efficiently** in bold letters. We were becoming overwhelmed with work, business, raising our son and life in general. The following day, we met at the airport and that evening we turned on our laptops to review our to-do lists. Since time management was on the list we discussed automation.

It's important to develop effective strategies for managing your time to balance your life and bring order to your daily activities. Time management skills are valuable for staying organized, reducing stress and relieving that feeling of being overwhelmed. Automation allows for more productivity and frees valuable time to let you concentrate on more important things.

Do you still pay bills by cheque or pay them manually online? Automate – arrange for payment to be automatically charged to your credit card or taken from your bank account each month. We have automated our municipal tax payments; our credit card payments; cell phone, water, gas and electricity bills; our mortgage payments; rental cheque deposits and more. Thanks to automation, we now spend only 15 to 30 minutes each week checking our accounts to ensure all is in order and on track.

Here is an example of what automation looks like in our lives: We wake up when our bodies and minds tell us to, which is normally around 8:00 AM. Our coffee is ready because we programmed the machine to brew it at 7:30. We have coffee and breakfast and turn on our computers to review our to-do list.

In our emails we've been copied on a message by Rose, our mortgage broker's assistant. She communicated with our bank regarding cheques for a second mortgage deal. We had introduced Rose and John, our bank customer service manager, to simplify and automate the process so we no longer have to be involved in those transactions. We have also received an email from Banco Nacional de Costa Rica confirming a bill payment – *luz y aqua* (electricity and water). An email from FlipKey confirms the transfer of a payment through our PayPal account for our rental unit in Costa Rica. Another email alerts us to a withdrawal made with our Interac card, suggesting we contact the bank if the transaction was not legitimate (it was – Daniel had just purchased a new suit). Multiple Listing Service (MLS) sent us a listing of potential homes for sale based on our criteria, automated following a request to our real estate agent because we want to keep up to date on trends in the housing market in our area.

Next, we access our bank account to glance at the activity for the past few days. We saw that the property taxes on our house in Toronto were paid in full. We also noticed another amount automatically withdrawn to pay off our credit card. Electrical and gas bill payments were also automatically withdrawn from our account for our homes and our cell phone bill was settled. Both insurance payments were also withdrawn. All mortgage payments also appeared. This is the beginning of the month, so we see that all our post-dated rental cheques were deposited into our account. It's rather reassuring to see money coming in! At a glance we could see that more money was coming in than going out so everything was on track and nothing had to be done thanks to our automation process. After answering a few emails we closed the laptops with a smile knowing everything was on schedule.

Another good reason to automate is that if you ever get sick or have to remove yourself from daily life because of some other emergency – or even take an extended vacation – bills would be paid and deposits would be made in your absence. You would know things would continue as usual and you wouldn't have to worry. Free your time to focus on more important or fun stuff. This is what being among the fortunate few is about!

We see automation as a virtual assistant. If you are going to be successful managing your life, your family, your job, your investments and perhaps multiple properties and projects, you must learn to be productive and understand time management and the importance of automation. It took us over a year to get all our ducks in a row and to get everything working without glitches. Implementing automation may be a little time consuming but think about the advantages and remember to associate it with pleasure, not pain! After it is set up, you never have to worry about being late on a payment or forgetting birthdays because your electronic calendar automatically reminds you. Decrease your level of involvement and micromanagement and encourage communication among your team members. This is entrepreneurship. There is no way you could keep up with all these tasks without automation – they would simply take over your life and you would be so overwhelmed and consumed with work and worry that you would simply give up on your plan.

Start now with whatever bill you have and gradually add to your own automation program. Work smarter from now on. Look at what consumes your time and delegate or automate.

Bill Gates once said that "automation applied to an inefficient operation will magnify the inefficiency." To be effective at automating you must also evaluate what is worth automating. Don't automate tasks that should be eliminated altogether.

Delegation

Delegation goes hand in hand with automation. Look for items on your to-do list, especially recurring ones you can delegate: hire people who can help you complete specific tasks.

We used to do our own accounting and bookkeeping. We still use a lot of spreadsheets but just as a way to make sure the automation process is on track. We now have an accountant do our bookkeeping, which relieves us of a demanding task and ensures that our taxes are done properly. We pride ourselves in having the best experts around us and we love to quiz our accountant on best practices and other tricks we should know about. Having our insurance broker look for the best insurance rates is also delegation. Delegation is part of what allows us time to do what's really important to us in life.

Here's another example of delegating: when doing our year-end report for our accountant, we need to supply the total insurance costs on all our properties. We used to go to our filing cabinet and pull out the files on all the properties. We would then have to flip through all the invoices in each file and pull out the insurance reports for each property. We then read through the totals and entered the data onto our spreadsheet. Reading insurance statements is not easy – they seem to be unnecessarily complicated, as if they don't want clients to figure out the real cost.

After spending an hour on this task, we thought there must be an easier way. We finally decided to ask our insurance broker to produce a report for all our properties. Brilliant! At the end of the day, our insurance broker's email came in and we had all the information we needed to send to our accountant to file our taxes.

This is just one instance. Many times, if we think about it and take a step back, we can reach the desired results with a little help. So don't be afraid to ask for it. The bottom line is being smart about your tasks and better at managing time-consuming and tedious work.

Setting Goals: The Multi-Year Plan

Do you know what you will have accomplished in your life 10 years from now? Most people don't. Why not? Because they don't have a plan. Make a plan, write it down and put it into action. Your plan is the road map to your goal, the blueprint to your success.

What follows is the most important message we can share with you to help you achieve success. Read carefully, apply this technique and you will be amazed at how efficient you have become and how quickly you will accomplish your goals.

Even though most people believe goal-setting is important, eight in 10 people say their life lacks an overall goal, according to Scott Sadler of Creative Conflict Solutions. For example, of people who make New Year's resolutions, only one in five actually writes them down. It isn't surprising that one in four people makes the same resolutions every year. Explicitly writing down your goal makes you 10 times more likely to achieve it.

Setting goals is worth it if you can commit to actually following your plan. To experience financial independence and long-term wealth, to take care of your health and your loved ones, to develop your spirituality, to travel or own a home in the Caribbean or a magnificent boat – whatever it is you desire – you must believe in the importance of having both a short-term and a long-term plan: we suggest creating a one-, two-, three-, five- and 10-year plan. Every month, look at your plan and make the necessary updates – see below. Your daily to-do lists are directly linked to this plan.

Everyone's individual plan is distinct, of course – you can't expect to follow or copy someone else's; you must develop your own. Yes, you can learn from someone else and use techniques others use, but your plan and your desires are your own and you will have to grant yourself time for reflection until you get a clear picture of your greater aspirations in life. Everyone's objectives are very different; one may have a large family and thus may want more money for music or dance lessons for their children. One may want to fly helicopters as a hobby and will therefore need a lot more money than the person who wants to live a simple life in a hut by the ocean. You may be lucky enough to have a considerable pension from your employer; others may have no pension plan. One person's long-term plan may be hindered by a long illness; someone else's might be catapulted by an unexpected inheritance.

Our plan is constantly affected by many factors and needs to be adapted throughout the 10-year period. For your plan to be relevant to your needs and wants, it needs to be an evolving document and you must review it regularly. Don't file it or leave it in a drawer, make it visible. You could have it posted on your bathroom mirror so you can see it every morning. You could have it on the back of your bedroom door or on your refrigerator, etc. You will get better at achieving your goals as you go and will likely be able to modify your plan to advance to the next level.

Let's talk about developing your plan. Some people use life coaches or financial planners, and this may be a good investment, but you can also create a plan on your own. Many planners and other resource people are part of companies that sell products (such as investment or software products). Be careful about who you choose to involve in your plan. We preferred to develop our own. We enjoy listening to the advice of people who have achieved success and we are always open to different approaches and techniques. If you prefer to seek professional guidance, we suggest you choose an independent advisor; your planner should focus on your needs and goals and should not have any personal motives or agenda, such as selling a product or additional services (the same principles apply to your stock broker). A life coach may help you ask yourself the right questions and deepen your thoughts on the kind of life you want and this can definitely set you on the right path.

Your plan will include many components, which will be detailed by following a set of five simple probes: what, when, where, why and how. Below are possible components of your plan:

- Finances
- Social life
- Health (physical and mental)
- Spirituality
- Family
- Education
- Profession/work
- Leisure
- Travel

On the next level, going into more detail, the finances section of your plan could be broken down into the following:

- Cash flow
- Net worth
- Expenses
- Savings
- Risk tolerance
- Investment strategies
- Tax situation
- Retirement goals

The social life components of your plan would probably include such elements as these:

- Relationship
- Family
- Friends

- Social gatherings
- Charitable work and activities

Creating your plan and detailing every aspect of it leads you to take control of your life and your future. By looking at where you are and where you want to be, you will begin to develop an action plan to reach each of your goals.

Time management is essential to achieving your goals. We used to-do lists to manage multiple properties and tenants while raising our son (including driving him to various activities), working full time, visiting families, doing household and yard chores, travelling, our weekly romantic dinner, etc.

If you have bad debt, such as credit card debt, getting rid of it has to be part of your plan. Rest assured there is a way out, but it takes planning. First, get a loan to pay off the credit card debt at half (or less) the interest rate your card charges and then make the largest payments you can on the loan – not just the required minimum but a substantial amount of the principal too. If you have equity against your home, apply for a line of credit against your home at even lower interest. Withdraw the amount owing on your credit card from the line of credit and pay off the card completely. Now make it a priority to put the maximum amount possible toward paying off the line of credit each month.

Make sure your financial plan allows you to pay off your credit card balance in total each and every month. One good practice in reaching financial independence or wealth is never paying interest on credit cards. There can be rare exceptions to this rule but generally, avoid credit card interest. For more information on planning, go to *TheFortunateFew.com.*

How to make your life plan

The first thing you have to do to engage in the planning process is brainstorm about your goals and desires. Imagine yourself in 10 years. How do you picture your life? Make this exercise effortless, interesting and fun. Sit in a peaceful, comfortable place where you will not be interrupted. Turn off your cell phone and start this exercise with deep breathing and, as you write, keep a smile on your face. Make sure you don't leave out any important elements of your life: finances, personal, education, health, spiritual, social, family, etc. Do not categorize items yet (this will come later) or self-edit, just list all your ideas on a piece of paper. This should be enjoyable and exciting!

Here's an example of what your first stream-of-consciousness list could look like.

- Three children
- Own a four-bedroom home
- Be a landlord
- Master's degree
- New car
- Boat
- Cottage
- Three investment homes
- Condo by the sea
- Management level at job
- Financial freedom
- Read one book per week
- Be truly happy
- Exercise three times a week
- Yoga
- Visit parents every second month
- Rental income
- RESP for the children's education
- Disney cruise with family
- Bike for cancer research

Once you have completed your list and feel satisfied with what you envision for your life, start grouping your ideas under more specific categories, such as finances, personal, education, health, social, family, etc. These categories will become sections when you transfer your wishes to the "What" section of your 10-year Life Planning Worksheet. Keep smiling!

This 10-year plan doesn't preclude you from having goals you want to reach sooner than 10 years: if you want to reach management level at work in your 10th year, you might need to do some professional development within the next five years, such as undertaking management training. To achieve financial independence, in your second year you might include in the "How" section reading books about the stock market so you understand how to invest in stocks.

It is surprising how quickly time flies. The whole purpose of this exercise is to make sure the next 10 years don't pass you by and to make sure they are the most productive years of your life as you set the foundation for your financial freedom. Remain aware as you start your plan that following it will mean dedication, perseverance and commitment. This plan should keep you productive and provide you with a sense of direction and accomplishment.

Description of terms

What: Your list of desires and wants (personal, material, professional, etc.).

Where: The place you will accomplish this task – for example, your promotion may take you to a different city, or you may know where you will get your management certificate so you would write the name of the specific institution in this column.

When: Your time frame – when you want to achieve a given task. For example, you want the management certificate in two years; if we are now in 2015, write 2017. This forces you to take the necessary steps before the "deadline" to accomplish this goal. The more precise the dates, the better.

Chapter 3

Why: This is what will generate the drive you need to accomplish a specific goal or desire. It motivates you because it connects your emotions to what you want. Why do you want your motorcycle licence? It is not receiving the licence itself that is the driving force behind this goal, it is the freedom it will give you, the independence and the enjoyment you will feel that will drive you to attain that goal.

How: A detailed description of the steps you will take to achieve your goal. For example, if the "What" is gaining a management certificate and the "When" is August 2016, the "How" could be to register at University XYZ to complete the certificate in eight months; devote two hours a day, five days a week, to studying, doing homework between 9 and 11 PM every evening after the kids are in bed. Be as specific and detailed as you can.

Your worksheet will evolve and change every year because the second year of your two-year plan will become the first year of your plan next year (with updates):

Your 10 year plan	1st year of plan is...	2nd year of plan is...	3rd year of plan is...	4th year of plan is...	5th year of plan is...	10th year of plan is...
Year 1	2016	2017	2018	—	2020	2025
Year 2	2017	2018	2019	2020	2021	2025
Year 3	2018	2019	2020	2021	2022	2025
Year 4	2019	2020	2021	2022	2023	2025
Year 5	2020	2021	2022	2023	2024	2025
Year 6	2021	2022	2023	2024	2025	—
Year 7	2022	2023	2024	2025	—	—
Year 8	2023	2024	2025	—	—	—
Year 9	2024	2025	—	—	—	—
Year 10	2025	—	—	—	—	—

Following the end of your first year (2016), you will rewrite your five-year plan because the fifth year now becomes the fourth year, and so on. This sounds complicated but once you start doing it you will realize how simple this task is and how important it is to keeping you on track in attaining all your goals.

Remember to keep your goals realistic. Doing so will allow you to accomplish and succeed and you won't get discouraged. Your evolving worksheet will take you places you never thought possible. On our worksheet, we had planned to acquire three investment properties within five years. To our surprise we achieved it in three years. We find that most of what we write down on our worksheet becomes reality before the "When" date we originally specified. This is encouraging and motivating for us. Our planning worksheet looks much different now than it did just a few years ago. Now, it is about where we want to travel, what activities we want to do, such as which castle we want to visit in Europe or what reef we want to snorkel. Surrender yourself to the possibilities. Love life and live the life you desire.

Below are sample Life Planning Worksheets. For this example, we've referred to goals we listed earlier in the chapter, but of course you will create a worksheet filled with your own individual goals. It is important to start with your 10-year goals because this will give you a clear vision of your future and will set a critical path to bring you to your objectives. The following sample worksheets (10-year, five-year and one-year) list the actions to reach these goals and include short-term goals as well.

We have detailed a few items in the finances, social life and health sections of each plan as examples, just to show you how the plan works, but of course your worksheet should include more "What" goals under all sections you create for your plan. Remember that this planning worksheet is personal – it will be different for everyone. As a couple, we did the exercise separately and amalgamated our plans afterward. Doing so was truly helpful in understanding each other's aspirations and was a great way to help each other attain our respective and common objectives.

Life Planning Worksheets

Sample 10-year plan (for 2025)

What (Goal)	When	Where	Why	How
Finances				
$120,000 annual income	2022–25	In an organization that will benefit from my expertise	To reach my goal of working at upper management/executive level, to help attain financial goals, to provide better lifestyle for me and family	Continue professional development, apply for and obtain position at upper management/executive level, add more details to job search
Rental income $2,000 per month net	2024–25	In a major city	To increase household income and diversify investment portfolio	Half of mortgage principal paid off by using accelerated biweekly payments and adding 10% against principal yearly as per mortgage agreement
Etc…				
Social Life				
Do Bike for Cancer Research for local hospital	Fall 2025	Hospital Bike for Cancer Research	To give back to commnity and fight to find cure for cancer, to make me a better person	Register, find sponsors and train for this event
Monthly gathering of friends	2015–25, last Friday of each month	To be determined (restaurant, coffee shop, home)	To meet with friends I cherish and love and stay grounded	Organize monthly gathering; research locations the Wednesday before, send email Thursday morning with place/time details
Etc…				
Health				
Become a yoga instructor	2021–25	Local yoga studio; offer sessions at home	To be in touch with myself and continue a healthy practice, to give back by offering my expertise to those who wish to receive it	Advertise in local media, on Internet and with sign in my neighbourhood and in front of my house
Eat healthy	2015–25	Locally, and by eating at home more often	To be healthy, have a stronger immune system, be an example to our children, live longer, feel good and enjoy good quality of life	Find farmers' markets and grocery stores that offer organic and local produce, find butcher or farmer who sells organic meat, search Internet, ask local produce people where to find best healthy produce
Spirituality				
Family				
Education				
Profession/work				
Leisure				
Travel				

Sample five-year plan (for 2020)

What (Goal)	When	Where	Why	How
Finances				
$80,000 annual income	2021	Within the same organization and other departments, if not available, search potential leads in different organizations	To attain my income level goal and continue to provide a better life for me and my family, to give me a sense of worth and self-esteem	Continue professional development and start MBA program, work on professional networking, use social media sites such as LinkedIn
Rental income from new investment property (break even)	2021	Metropolitan area	To reach our financial goals by becoming landlords, owning property as an investment	Have rental income cover mortgage and expenses, find good-quality rental property, find good tenants
Etc…				
Social Life				
Do Bike for Cancer Research for local hospital	Fall 2021	Hospital Bike for Cancer Research	To give back to commnity and fight to find cure for cancer, to make me a better person	Register, find sponsors and train for this event, allocate 2 days a week to finding sponsors and practise biking 30 km
Monthly gathering of friends	2021–25, last Friday of each month	To be determined each month	To foster the beautiful friendship that exists, it gives me pleasure to be in their presence, they are a great support group	Organize monthly gathering; research locations the Wednesday before, send email Thursday morning with place/time details
Etc…				
Health				
Become a yoga instructor	2021	Local studio	To be in touch with myself and remain healthy	Register for Yoga Teaching Training program
Eat healthy	2021–25	Home – make the right choices no matter where we are, eat at restaurants less often	To be an example to my children, to live healthy lifestyle so I can have energy and stamina to accomplish dreams and goals	Find organic produce and meats
Family				
Education				
Profession/work				
Leisure				
Travel				

Chapter 3

Sample one-year plan (for 2015)

What (Goal)	When	Where	Why	How
Finances				
Increase annual income to $50,000	2016	Present place of employment	To pay bills, feed family and start saving a little	Continue working at present job while looking at training possibilities
Open TFSA	2016	My bank	To contribute and have my investment grow tax free to save to invest in income property	Have monthly automated withdrawals and invest any additional money I save, take on side contracts to maximize investments to save down payment to purchase first income property first income property
Etc…				
Social Life				
Monthly gathering of friends	2016, last Friday of each month	To be determined each month	We love our friends and want to make time to see them more often	Allocate time to invite friends for monthly get-together
Etc…				
Health				
Yoga	2016	Local studio	Stay in touch with myself, relieve stress, keep healthy	Register for yearly membership, go at least twice a week
Eat healthy	2016	At home and when eating out	I want to be healthy for my kids, I care about my health	Quit social smoking, eat more vegetables, cut down on carbs and sugar
Family				
Education				
Profession/work				
Leisure				
Travel				

By studying these Life Planning Worksheets closely, you will notice, for example, that the yoga certification is listed on the 10-year plan but does not appear on the one-year plan. It showed up later in the planning because it was not a priority for the first few years. Also note the changes to the income goal, increasing over the years to reach the $120,000 goal. The increase in salary (from $50,000 to $80,000) is linked to education and professional development activities such as the management certification. Note, however, that the $80,000 to the $120,000 salary jump is linked to the MBA, which would be detailed in the education section of your plan.

Downloads for Life Planning Worksheets are available here: *http://www.thefortunatefew.com/tools-and-resources/*

A Few Fortunate Thoughts about Time Management and Planning

- Sit down and work specifically on your future. Envisioning where you would like to be in 10 years might not be easy – it means deliberately examining your life. Start brainstorming: where do you want to be next year? In five years? In 10? Start writing and developing your plan.

- Scrutinize how your day is structured. Has your work schedule taken over your life or have you made time to work on what is really important to you? Daily to-do lists will ensure you get both your professional and personal work done. Make sure your list includes elements that will take you toward your goals.

- Be productive. Identify what can help you manage your time. Change old habits. Eliminate negative time consumers.

- Take a close look at the way you manage bill payments, bank transactions, etc. Automate all your payments and other routine functions. Delegate tasks to experts around you and outsource when necessary. With the resulting free time, review your life plan weekly. Involve your partner to bring convergence to your visions.

Chapter 4
Surround Yourself with Experts: Build Your Team

Great things in business are never done by one person. They're done by a team of people.

Steve Jobs

A night on the town, Naples, Florida

Naples is the crown jewel of Southwest Florida, nestled on the sun-drenched beaches of the Gulf of Mexico. It is known for world-class shopping and dining and abundant, challenging golf courses. It is also only steps from seclusion on Keewaydin Island, with the untamed tropical wilderness of the Everglades. That part of the Floridian coast offers one of the US's best sandboxes and calmest seas.

We decided to support a good cause by purchasing tickets to a fundraising dance for a local hospital charity. So we dressed up in our clubbing gear and started downtown on the famous 5th Avenue South, filled with shops, restaurants and cafés, a soothing breeze coming from the Gulf of Mexico. We had dinner at Café Luna, chatting, laughing, savouring good food and wine. We then strolled along the main street, shopping and visiting art galleries.

As the sun set and the evening was progressing, we made our way to the charity event at about 11:00 PM. There we found an amazing band composed of guitars, piano, saxophones and singers. The event was set up in a huge white tent with a large stage, with everything decorated to create a great atmosphere. We were ready to party. We danced until closing and had a fantastic time. We hailed a cab and watched Naples' lights dim as we headed back to the condo, comfortably cuddled in the back seat.

Chapter 4

A night out, Naples, USA.

Surround Yourself with Experts: Build Your Team

When we chose to spend an evening out in Naples, we could have chosen any concert hall or restaurant but decided to participate in a good cause: contributing to a fund to build a garden for cancer patients at the local treatment centre. We felt connected to that community that evening, part of something greater than the two of us. We need others in life, we need companionship, we need expertise to complement our own abilities and experts to help us make the right decisions. Create your dream team!

Building Your Team

We searched for many years before we found all the key members of our team, the ones we feel are the right people for us to work with. We would not be able to live the life we do if it were not for their expertise and guidance.

As with any business relationship, some experts have worked with us for a while and moved on as our needs changed and as we needed to learn more, evolve and further accomplish the steps in our plan. Our current team is made up of a lawyer, a real estate specialist, a mortgage broker, an accountant, our webmaster, our property manager in Costa Rica and, most recently, our bank manager, who has become crucial to ensuring our affairs run smoothly while we are out of the country.

Team members, unlike consultants hired for a specific, limited task, have to understand your vision and your goals. They become collaborators. We feel we can call on our team members anytime to get their input. Our lawyer signs off on our real estate deals and partnership agreements and gives us advice when we need it. Our real estate specialist helps us find properties by automatically emailing us daily lists of properties for sale based on our criteria. Our mortgage broker sets up our mortgages and makes sure they are at the best rates and set up to our advantage. He also puts together second mortgage deals and presents them to us as investment opportunities. Our webmaster ensures that our websites are kept current with security updates, functions for rental calendars and pop-ups for advertisements and makes sure the sites show up in web browsers. Our property manager makes sure clients who rent our homes in Costa Rica have everything they need to be happy and enjoy their vacation; she also maintains the properties. She collects the rental fees and supervises and pays our gardener, pool maintenance people and house cleaners. Our bank manager understands our business as well as our lifestyle and has found a way to tailor services to our needs with simple systems for tasks such as ensuring cheques are deposited in the right accounts every month. Our team members know us quite well and we are also interested in what they do. We are in constant communication with them and regularly take time to go out for a coffee or dinner with them to maintain a healthy professional relationship.

Realistically, it takes time to find and put together team members like these. You will likely see many come and go before you finally feel comfortable letting them into your circle.

Let us be clear about a few things. Some professionals – lawyers practising in family, civil or commercial law, for example – may tend to take over your case. Sometimes the decisions they make are in their best interest and not yours. It is important to clearly communicate your objectives and make sure your team members are always working toward those goals. You are paying for their service and you should feel they are listening to you and understand your needs. They should not take over your affairs but rather put their expertise at your service. We seek and appreciate their professional advice but don't allow their ease in their milieu to take over. We have dealt with a few lawyers in the past and we like to clearly set our intentions early in our relationship to avoid wasting time and resources. Be clear on your objectives, their fees and timelines for transactions.

Accountants are also important. Don't take their knowledge for granted. Daniel's father gave us good advice about accountants: it's good to change every three or four years because you can learn a lot from an accountant. By changing, you can access new insight and great advice on new strategies. That being said, if you have a truly great accountant, you might not want to change. Like lawyers, who specialize in different types of litigation, accountants also specialize so try to find one who knows your business.

Partners

Having your soul mate as a partner

If you are in a good, loving long-term relationship, you're in luck. Your partner holds half the promise to your success as you hold half of theirs. Welcome his or her abilities and genuine commitment to your joint plan and don't take what your partner has to offer for granted. Include this natural ally in your business plan and you will speed up your success. Make sure your plan reflects both your dreams and aspirations. As mentioned in Chapter 3, you should each develop your own plan and then amalgamate the two.

Of course, we were not always in business together. At the end of the 1990s, we both owned homes with different partners. In one case, real estate was purchased in partnership with multiple business partners – three work colleagues. That partnership lasted less than five years before one partner announced he was relocating to another province to advance his career. This unexpected move forced the group to sell their four properties and liquidate all their investments.

When this happened, we decided to go into business together. This, of course, worked out very well for us because we did not have to share the profits with anyone else. And when you're in business with your soul mate, you're working on the same goals, which brings understanding and motivation to both.

But developing a business relationship with your spouse does not exclude other possible partnerships. For example, if you and your spouse don't have the cash for the down payment for a real estate purchase, an outside partner or two can help. We started investing in real estate with other partners, which laid the foundation for us to continue that success.

Other partners

Choose your partners wisely! A bad choice could completely undermine your plan. Yes, partnerships have been the foundation for successful businesses but they can also become a source of stress. Some abide by the golden rule of business, "Never go into business with family or friends," because doing so can indeed ruin your relationships. If you are considering a family member as a partner, know that there is a possibility that your relationship will change drastically. If you want to protect or maintain the relationship you have, reconsider your decision. In our opinion, having your spouse as your business partner is a great option because you have common goals and are working together to achieve your destiny as a team. That's a great formula.

Let's take a look at the pros and cons of having a partner other than your spouse. On a positive note, having a partner other than your spouse allows you to:

- Share expenses, risk and responsibilities to lessen the stress
- Increase the pool of expertise and skills
- Gain access to more capital
- Have more leads and contacts
- Develop a support system and build motivation, drive and enthusiasm
- Have freedom in terms of time off

On the negative side, having a partner other than your spouse means you must:

- Share the profits
- Reconcile different visions when making decisions
- Face possible dissolution of the business if a partner leaves
- Put more effort into communication
- Take more time for decision-making and consultation

How do you choose your partner?

How you choose a partner depends on you as much as on your prospective partner. It depends on your personality, your approach, your ability to give and take and so on. Consider the following when choosing a business partner: if you prefer to make all the decisions yourself, with a "my way or the highway" attitude and you are simply looking for a partner to finance your project, a silent partner may be a good option for you.

A business partner should complement your own abilities – for example, if communication is not your forte, finding a partner who is a good communicator is crucial. In business you need to be a good communicator and you need to be able to deal with different people in various situations. If you lack negotiation skills, have a partner who is skilled in that area. Is your partner able to handle conflict or are you better in dealing with challenges? You also need to consider the balance of power (decision-making) within your partnership, along with values, ethics and personalities. You therefore need to know yourself pretty well to be able to choose the right partners to complement your skills and mesh with your personality and values.

It's important to know as much as possible about a potential partner before signing on the dotted line, because his or her finances and family life may affect the business. You both need to answer these questions:

- Do you share the same vision and level of commitment?
- Are you clear on the partnership agreement?
- What are your expectations of the time involved?
- Are you clear about your individual responsibilities?
- Do you have an exit strategy if things go wrong?
- What is your partner's reputation in the community?
- Do you respect each other?
- Do you have a good feeling about your relationship?

Our advice is that you put the terms of partnerships with anyone other than your spouse in writing and clarify all responsibilities and how financing will be organized. If your prospective partner is not willing to put everything in writing, this should be a red flag. Even if your partner is your spouse, much discussion on the subject and good communication are essential. You are in it together.

Like a marriage, it is easier to go into a partnership than it is to get out of one. The best time to address potential problems with your partner is at the beginning, before emotions run high. It is obviously impossible for you to predict every problem that could arise, but ask your lawyer and maybe your accountant to review your partnership agreements to make sure the framework you have in place can help address unforeseen circumstances.

To conclude, a partnership can increase your chances for success and can be a great experience, but it can also be the opposite. So take your time, communicate openly with prospective partners, do your research and protect yourself to make sure your partnership is a positive one.

Real Estate Agents

Although we have learned about the real estate trade and built our success on it, we don't agree with how the real estate profession protects and controls the market to make money, as a monopoly would. We feel it is our right to sell our home ourselves if we choose to. We believe sellers should decide for themselves whether to use a realtor or not. We are happy that there has been some change in the old system and that the MLS must now accept listings from people who are selling their properties without an agent.

When we listed our principal home in Richmond Hill, Ontario, for sale on our own, our colleague and friend, a realtor we had always used in the past, was furious and could not hide his disappointment. We had bought and sold many properties with his help and he had made a lot of money with us. This time around, we needed to maximize our profit to reach our objective. We decided to offer him a 1% commission as the listing agent, take it or leave it. Finally, and with a lot of discontentment, he accepted, although clearly unhappy. He was well aware that because of regulations in his profession there was no way for us to avoid paying the realtor who brought the buyers to us the required 2.5%, so he was getting the short end of the stick.

Chapter 4

For homeowners, there are pros and cons to using a realtor. By cutting out the middle person and selling your home yourself, you can save thousands, even tens of thousands, of dollars. First, without a realtor, you will save on average 5% to 6% of the value of the sale on commission. So if you sell your home for $300,000, that's up to $18,000 in savings. If your home is worth double that, you would save $36,000 with commission fees at 6%. If you're selling your principal residence, that $36,000 goes directly into your pocket tax free.

Some believe it's essential to have the expertise of a realtor, but times have changed. We no longer need a realtor to drive us from house to house. We now let our computer travel with the powerful tool of the Internet. We have access to the resources and information we need to find or sell a property. We have found most of the homes we've purchased ourselves. The only times we call our realtor is to book an appointment to see the home if the owner selling the home has listed it with an agent. You can also call the listing agent directly and negotiate a decrease in their commission if you don't have a realtor to represent you. In this case, if the listing agent is business minded, he or she will agree to a better commission rate, to your advantage. If not, bring in your agent and negotiate a return of some sort with the agent representing you. This could be in the form of a gift, so to speak. Business is business.

If you're selling, you can now advertise your own home on many websites, as the Ontario MLS has finally allowed owners to market and advertise their properties on what used to be an exclusive tool for realtors. Also investigate other sites specializing in advertising homes for sale, such as _ComFree.com_, _PropertyGuys.com_ and _ForSaleByOwner.com_. Homeowners no longer need an agent to get their properties seen by prospective buyers.

It is also key to understand that realtors are not property appraisers; determining the value of your house is not necessarily their area of expertise. You can hire a professional appraiser, which will cost you about $300. Most appraisers reach a value through three methods, which should be combined. The first is the cost approach: what would it cost to replicate the house in its current location? The second is the sales comparison analysis and the third is the income method, typically used if the home is in an area with a lot of rental properties or government-funded housing, also known as co-op housing.

When a realtor estimates the value of a home, he or she does the same analysis we do ourselves: looking on MLS for comparable homes – those that resemble yours and are in a similar area. Undertaking that research yourself is the best way to learn about the real estate market.

If you're selling a commercial property, you might need a realtor because some commercial sale contracts can be more technical and complex. Agents that are true experts in their field can offer good advice and deal with important elements you may overlook on your own.

At closing, your most important advisor is the real estate lawyer who will finalize the paperwork. Realtors can't legally sign off on legal documents attesting to the sale and the new title on the house. A real estate lawyer will ensure that the documents pertaining to the sale are in order and will verify that everything is legal. You can easily find a real estate lawyer who can handle the legal aspects of your purchase or sale, such as ensuring there are no outstanding liens (claims against debt) against the property.

If you are willing to make the effort of setting appointments to view homes for sale or to show your own home, and if you are willing to look for a real estate lawyer, you will save 5% to 6% on the cost of selling. So pay yourself $36,000 on your $600,000 property. That sounds good, doesn't it?

Banking

It is important that you chose a bank that will work for you. You have to look at fees, interest charged and earned, the services and

Chapter 4

products offered, the staff's level of competence and professionalism and more. For us, a National Bank of Canada All-In-One account was the best choice. Instead of having savings just sitting in our account, our money automatically goes toward our debt. However, we deal with multiple banking institutions, such as Scotia Bank, Bank of Montreal and Olympia Trust, to name a few. This allows us leveraging and negotiating power when we need to deal with our bank. We'll talk more about bank accounts in the next chapter.

We have always made a point of meeting with the bank manager every time we are shopping for a new mortgage or a new bank. It is important for us to connect with this key person and that she or he knows us. We take time to explain what it is we do and the type of service we require. We make an effort to go to our bank in person to maintain that contact.

A Few Fortunate Thoughts about Building Your Team

- Acknowledge that you need expertise from others to realize your objectives. This means being able to clearly communicate your vision while searching for the right collaborators until you find a good fit.

- Choose your partners wisely. In a true partnership, each individual's weaknesses are alleviated by the other's strengths.

- Having your soul mate as a partner can facilitate communication and allows you to focus on the same goals, thus fast tracking your progress and connecting you in celebrating successes. There is no greater sense of satisfaction than knowing you achieved your goals together.

- Learn real estate. This might mean you settle your first few deals paying full commission to your real estate agent. As you learn the ropes, consider selling or buying a home yourself. Have a good lawyer look at the sales or purchase agreements before closing. If you prefer to use the services of a real estate agent, know that his or her expertise comes at a cost.

- Meet with the bank managers in your area. Share your goals and let them explain why their institution is the best for you. Banks are becoming more customer oriented and offer more products than ever before. Choose one (or more) that offers products, services and fees that satisfy your business needs. We use many banks to get everything we need.

Chapter 5
How We Did It: The Winning Formula

It's not where you start – it's where you finish that counts.

Zig Ziglar

Morning yoga, Negril, Jamaica

Carole

One of my dearest friends from Vancouver was getting married: it would be our first "destination wedding" and first visit to Jamaica, the third-largest island of the Greater Antilles. We spent a lot of time together looking at pictures of beautiful 7 Mile Beach in Negril with its white sand and contrasting dark reefs. And off we went!

We found a yoga centre just across from the wedding venue and decided to rent a cabin and make a Zen vacation out of this one-week getaway. Our cabin was made of whitewashed wood with its own private garden in front of the entrance, where we would enjoy our morning coffee accompanied by a cute little black cat named Gandhi. We headed to the yoga platform for the 9:00 am session instructed by Fanette, a French yogini, who skilfully led us through our morning sun salutations. The wooden structure was a stunning palapa with a spacious, shiny bamboo floor and an impressive roof made of thousands of palm leaves, perfectly woven. What a wonderful way to start the day in this oasis of calm, where the aroma of flowers and coffee floated around us while we stretched and moved our bodies in harmony!

We then savoured our breakfast with gratefulness and a good appetite. Maggie, the resident cook, prepared the most delicious banana pancakes. Off to 7 Miles Beach we went for our morning stroll, hand in hand and blissfully happy.

Waiting for us on the beach with the most brilliant smile and dreadlocks was Henry. It was a perfect day to go out on the jet ski! Daniel looked at me, daringly, and I just laughed, kicking off my sandals… let's do it! As directed by Henry, we rode the waters along the shore, found many caves to explore, and spotted the pink castle built right on the edge of a cliff. The ocean was bumpy and my arms were tightly wrapped around Daniel's waist as he drove his toy through the waves. The perspective from ashore was astounding, the colours of the small tropical homes, the trees, the reefs, sand and different shades of water were just perfectly balanced – the sun was shining brightly and we were charmed, ready to discover more of Jamaica's treasures.

Chapter 5

Jet skiing, 7 Mile Beach, Jamaica

We were able to leave on the spur of the moment to go to our friend's wedding in Jamaica. We don't take this freedom – or the fact that we have the means to pay for such a trip – for granted. This wasn't always the case and we never took a trip we couldn't afford. Avoiding bad debt has been one of our basic guiding principles.

Here we share other elements to guide your journey toward financial freedom.

Chapter 5

Our Formula for Success

We have created a formula for success and freedom that works for us and gladly share it with you. In this chapter, we tell you about the strategies and products we use to achieve the lifestyle we have. You may discover that you have already completed some of the steps!

Our basic formula is this:

1. Secure good employment.
2. Save for a down payment on a property using TFSAs and RRSPs.
3. Find the best mortgage broker in town.
4. Purchase your first principal home after completing Step 2.
5. Set up accelerated biweekly mortgage payments.
6. Build equity in your home and continue Step 2.
7. Open an All-In-One or similar account; foster a good relationship with your bank.
8. After completing Step 2 again, purchase a second home as an investment property and rent it out; repeat Step 5.
9. Continue saving and investing as much as you can in your RRSP and TFSA or toward your mortgage (depending on your tax bracket; see Chapter 8).
10. Open an account that allows you to invest your RRSP in second mortgage investments and mortgage investment corporations (MICs). Maximize your investment in second mortgages using a reliable mortgage broker, earning at least 8%.
11. Diversify your investments into at least four categories, such as MICs, individual stocks and mutual funds, real estate and miscellaneous investments of your choice (bonds, precious metals, etc.).

12. Once you have built up equity in your two homes, have the bank assess their market value and open a home equity line of credit (HELOC) within your All-In-One account against your equity.

13. Begin using the Smith Manoeuvre with your HELOC (see Chapter 6).

14. Purchase a third property (applying Steps 2, 5 and 12) and continue the process. Put investment income in your All-In-One account to increase the funds available in your HELOC and re-invest.

15. Continue using this formula until you've reached your goal – you could be well on your way in becoming a millionaire or even a multi-millionaire.

Each step is explained in more detail below; see Chapter 6, Equity is Power, for further discussion of the Smith Manoeuvre and Chapter 9, Investing, for more on different types of investment vehicles.

1. Obviously having **good employment** is important to get you started on your quest for financial freedom. Banks love people who are employed in well-paying jobs and they will happily grant these people a mortgage or lend them money. They are not as fond of those who are self-employed, and they are not at all interested in unemployed people. There are some exceptions, but in most cases these are the facts.

Banks and other lenders all want a guarantee that you are reliable, that you can be trusted and that you will be able to pay them back. Working for a company that has a good reputation and is not about to close up shop makes lenders comfortable. The higher your wages the better, but even if you are an average earner, as we were for years, it can work. A career in the public service or with para-public organizations is always a plus – there isn't much chance that the police force will shut down; the same goes for school boards, healthcare organizations, fire departments and other essential services. That's not to say that cutbacks can't happen, but generally, lending institutions perceive less risk when dealing with these types of employers. Working for very large companies such as banks, oil companies and auto makers can be just as beneficial.

Getting a mortgage if you're self-employed or retired is not as easy as it is if you've been traditionally well-employed for the past 10 years. This fact places young retirees, and those who are starting their careers, in a difficult position if they want to become active in the real estate market.

2. We won't go into too much detail on **saving for a down payment** in TFSAs and RRSPs because we cover this topic in Chapter 8. For now we'll just remind you how fortunate we are as Canadians to have access to these powerful tools to help us reach our objectives. Tax-free savings accounts are savings or investment accounts in which we can invest up to $5,500 a year. All earned interest is tax free – this means it's clear profit for you. Registered retirement savings plans, on the other hand, were created to help Canadians fund their retirement. Funds placed and earned in the account are not taxed until you withdraw them, when you will likely be in a lower tax bracket. Both are great vehicles to create wealth if used properly. The key is to maximize your contributions to both and to purchase high-earning investments within the plans.

3. Finding an excellent **mortgage broker** who understands your goals and objectives is crucial to the success of this formula. Your broker must be someone who can help you get the best mortgage rates possible for your real estate investments. We are the first to admit that our broker has helped us in many ways. He has become a key member of our team both as a mortgage broker and as a real estate financial advisor. He has been instrumental in our quest, answering our questions and tailoring mortgages to our needs. He has sound judgment, is down to earth, listens well and shares his knowledge. His advice has proven to be extremely valuable to us. Find yourself a broker you feel comfortable with, who understands your objectives, who's passionate about what he or she does and above all, who is highly competent.

4. Purchase your first **principal home.** Your principal home is where you reside most of the time; it is the largest investment most people will ever make. Once you buy a home you will no longer be giving your money away to a landlord and will be investing in yourself and your own portfolio. This purchase will lay the groundwork for your new career as an investor. As you continue making mortgage payments you will be building equity, which will give you the leverage to continue your journey toward freedom by following the investment plan you should by now have created as part of your Life Planning Worksheet.

5. Set up **accelerated biweekly mortgage payments.** Below is an example of monthly, semi-monthly and accelerated biweekly mortgage payments. In this example we use the following scenario.

Mortgage amount	$100,000
Interest rate	5%
Amortization period	25 years
Monthly mortgage payment	$581.60

Monthly mortgage payments simply mean you make payments once per month – that is, 12 payments per year. Based on the above scenario, the total mortgage payment annually is $6,979.20 ($581.60 × 12). With this monthly payment plan, it will take 25 years to pay off your mortgage.

Semi-monthly mortgage payments are made on the 1st and the 15th of every month. That means you make 24 payments per year. To figure out your payment plan, you simply divide the monthly payment by two ($581.60 ÷ 2 = $290.80). Based on this scenario, the total mortgage payment annually is $6,979.20 ($290.80 × 24), the same as if you made monthly payments of $581.60. Semi-monthly payments generate very little in savings. You will save some because you are paying down the principal a bit faster by paying twice per month instead of once per month.

Chapter 5

Accelerated biweekly mortgage payments, however, do exactly what they say – accelerate the payment of your mortgage. How? With semi-monthly payments you make 24 payments annually. With accelerated biweekly payments you make 26 payments annually. The difference is that you pay every two weeks (26 payments per year) instead of twice per month (24 payments per year). To figure out your payment plan, you divide the monthly mortgage payment by two and multiply it by 26 (every two weeks). In this scenario your total annual mortgage payment is $7,560.80: ($581.60 ÷ 2 = $290.80) × 26.

The savings using this method are substantial. You essentially make an extra monthly payment every year (the difference between $7,560.80 and $6,979.20 is $581.60). Using accelerated biweekly mortgage payments will save you money on interest and reduce your amortization period.

	Monthly payments	Biweekly payments	Accelerated biweekly payments
Mortgage amount	$100,000	$100,000	$100,000
Interest rate	5.00%	5.00%	5.00%
Amortization period	25 years	25 years	21.4 years
Mortgage payment	$581.60	$290.80 (× 24)	$290.80 (× 26)
Interest paid	$74,481.49	$74,301.97	$62,044.18
Savings	—	$179.52	$12,437.31

Looking at the difference between semi-monthly payments and accelerated biweekly payments, the savings in interest costs are substantial. The savings with semi-monthly payments over 25 years are just $179.52, whereas the accelerated biweekly payment savings are $12,437.31. Accelerated biweekly payments also reduce your amortization period from 25 years to 21.4 years. Adding the Smith Manoeuvre to accelerated biweekly payments can reduce your amortization period from 21.4 years to as little as 17 years. Use as many ways as possible to reduce the time it takes to pay off your mortgage and fast track your success.

6. **Build equity** in your home. As you'll read in the next chapter, equity is power. You can harness that power by making your mortgage payments rigorously to reduce the principal portion of your mortgage month after month and by making lump-sum payments against the mortgage whenever you can. The market value of your home plays an important part in the equity you have: if the value of your property increases, the equity in your home increases proportionately. Renovations can also increase your home's value and therefore your equity value. The higher the net worth of your property, the greater the equity you can leverage to borrow against it, using that borrowed money to invest. In most cases, your home is your most valuable asset and you can use the equity you build to meet ongoing credit needs and continue investing throughout your life.

7. Open an **All-In-One** or similar account. Choose the bank that best suits your needs and works to your advantage. The All-In-One banking option is offered by the National Bank of Canada, but several other banks offer this type of banking, including Royal Bank of Canada (Homeline Plan), Scotiabank (Scotia Total Equity Plan), Manulife (Manulife One) and Bank of Montreal (Homeowner Readiline). All these accounts work on the concept that your salary and any other deposits go immediately against your debt rather than sitting in a chequing account doing nothing, earning very little interest (if any). This system is the opposite of what we were used to in North America – it's not about showing you how much money you've saved but rather how much money you owe. In other words, you won't necessarily see a positive savings balance in your account unless you no longer have any debt. The system allows you to use funds as you would with any other account as long as you honour your monthly payments. Why is it smart to have your deposits go automatically toward your debt? Because it helps you pay down your debt faster and you pay less interest in the long run.

Here's a concrete example of the ingenuity of this product compared with a traditional mortgage. Let's say you have a regular mortgage loan of $200,000. You make your usual payments of $820 a month. Of that, $600 goes toward interest and $220 toward your principal. Your net pay (say $1,200 every two weeks) is automatically deposited into your chequing account. After your mortgage payment is deducted, you have $1,580 at your disposal. You need to reserve $800 for living expenses for the next month, leaving $780 sitting in your account earning nothing and saving you nothing while you are paying large amounts of interest on your debt. With an All-In-One account this $780 goes immediately against the debt. When this happens with every pay deposit, you save thousands in interest and pay down your mortgage much sooner.

8. **Purchase a second home** as an investment property. There are many benefits to having a second property in your portfolio. You can use it to build equity, just as you do with your principal residence, notably by having tenants pay down your mortgage (and because your tenants are essentially paying your mortgage, you don't need huge salaries to carry two or more mortgages). The ideal situation is to earn positive cash flow in addition to covering your mortgages and expenses. Remember that purchasing a property in a desirable location enhances your rental opportunities and your likelihood of profiting from a healthy real estate market. Don't forget that you can claim renovation and other costs related to the property as expenses on your income tax and that improvements to the property also increase its equity value. There's more on this in Chapter 9, Investing.

9. **Continue saving** by maximizing your RRSP contributions and taking advantage of your TFSA (see Chapter 8, Saving). If at all possible, make an extra payment (lump sum) toward your principal home's mortgage every year. Doing so can save you months of interest and considerably shorten the amortization period. It is possible to pay off your mortgage without much added stress in 17 years, rather than the usual 25 (see Chapter 9, Investing). Paying off the mortgage on your principal residence is your key to freedom. Keep everything in balance and stay on top of your credit card or any

other high-interest loan.

10. Open a **second mortgage investment account** with a financial institution that offers this type of product. Although financial institutions in Canada are allowed to offer MICs or second mortgage investments for RRSP investments, most banks don't offer this option. Olympia Trust and B2B Bank are a couple of institutions that offer self-directed registered plans (RRSPs, RESPs, RRIFs, etc.) through which you can invest in MICs and second mortgages. If you transfer all or part of your RRSP, for example, into a self-directed account, you will be able to invest in such high-interest-earning vehicles as second mortgages. Profits from investment are taxable as income unless the investments are in a registered plan and profits are re-invested directly into the plan; these earnings are not considered "contributions" to your registered plan.

Maximize your investment in second mortgages using your HELOC. For this type of investment, we lend money for second mortgages at an interest rate higher than what we pay on the money we withdrew from our HELOC, usually earning us between 8% and 12%. The borrowers secure their loan by using their home as collateral, minimizing our risk. Our mortgage broker is the driving force behind this technique. There are no setup costs for us as investors. All administration costs are assumed by the borrower and these mortgage contracts are prepared by lawyers. See Chapter 9, Investing, for more information on second mortgage investments.

11. Diversify your investments. We have diversified our portfolio into five types of investments:

- Real estate (safe)
- Second mortgage investments (moderate risk)
- MICs (safe)
- A few individual stocks and mutual funds (higher risk)
- Miscellaneous investments such as bonds, money market funds, Canadian securities (risk varies)

Chapter 5

In Chapter 9, we discuss how we allocate our money into each category.

We are comfortable with our investment choices and they work for us. Some would argue that real estate is not a "safe" investment – there are endless stories about people who have lost their money in real estate. We also lost on a real estate investment, a condo-hotel development with a golf course in Aylmer, Quebec. This deal ended up being challenged in both the civil and criminal courts. A bit more research on our part on the "developer" would have been enough to steer us away: he had been in jail for fraud. Nonetheless, a friend who had been successful in business had already invested in the development and we blindly followed his lead. This was an important lesson for us. Although we still feel real estate is a safe investment, it is important to diversify your investments to mitigate the risk if a catastrophe should occur.

12. Open a **HELOC**, which is a line of credit you can obtain if you have built up equity in your home. The financial institution that grants you the credit will recognize the equity in your home as security against your loan – or collateral. You will then have the freedom to use funds from your HELOC for such things as paying off high-interest student loans or credit card debt, for home renovations and for investing in second mortgages with the Smith Manoeuvre.

13. The **Smith Manoeuvre** is a technique that converts your regular non-tax-deductible mortgage payments into tax-deductible debt by using your home equity to borrow funds to invest. Using this technique can help you pay off your principal mortgage significantly faster. See the next chapter for details.

14. Purchase a **third property.** Now you can use your HELOC to make a down payment to invest in a third home or a commercial property. All expenses can be claimed on your taxes – even the down payment will be tax deductible. The tenants will pay rent, which will cover your mortgage payments and slowly but surely, you will start building equity in this new property.

Using the Smith Manoeuvre, continue to pay off your debts and increase equity in your properties. Use your HELOC to make investments that yield at least double the bank's rate of interest on your HELOC. In other words, if your bank charges 3.5% interest on the money you pull from your line of credit, you must look for investment with at least an 8% return. This is our general rule. Continue depositing all income – your salary, rental income, interest gains, etc., – in your unified account, thus increasing the amount of your HELOC available for reinvestment.

15. **Continue with this formula** – saving, investing, diversifying your investments and using these powerful tools (RRSPs, TFSAs, a unified bank account, a HELOC, the Smith Manoeuvre and second mortgage and MIC investments) – and you will soon be among the fortunate few!

A Few Fortunate Thoughts about the Winning Formula

- Create a formula you believe in and that will work for you. You may need to tweak it along the way but create a winning formula that you know deep down will drive you.

- Learn from others. When you are creating your own formula, let those who have succeeded inspire you. Incorporate elements from your 10-year plan, such as the "how," into your formula.

- Don't hesitate, don't procrastinate, don't second guess your talents. Just do it.

- Your formula may be different from ours; there may be elements you are already doing and others that might take a few months to set up. Be disciplined and keep working at it until you fully develop your own framework for success.

Chapter 6
Equity Is Power: Build It and Invest

Success is a mixture of skills, competence, luck and hard work: with a bit of effort, I believe the world can be at our feet.

Julie Payette

What happens in Vegas...

Our trip to Las Vegas on Daniel's 40th birthday remains the most vivid of our three visits to that city – everything was new and we were celebrating. While we waited at the airport in Toronto, we met a man by the name of Denis. We had a lot in common, so conversation was easy and interesting and we soon started talking about our families, books we had read and our goals in life. Denis was heading to a conference in Vegas. He'd been there often and knew the city of lights well.

Whenever we could, we would meet – by the pool for strawberries and champagne, at a world-renowned sushi restaurant or at the cigar lounge for a nightcap. Making friends along our journey is one of our most rewarding experiences. We joined Denis for a few Cirque du Soleil shows. We enjoyed the acrobatics showcased in O (water) but recommend Zumanity, a cabaret-style show that offers a seductive twist on reality. Quite an unforgettable show.

When Denis learned it was Daniel's birthday, he took it upon himself to treat us to an unforgettable evening: a party at Club 54 with a VIP booth. Daniel still raves about the VIP setting, the number of waitresses assigned to our table alone and the entertainment with scantily clad women who came down from the ceiling hanging on large hoops. It was an amazing night, like something right out of a movie. We were truly spoiled and remain grateful for Denis's friendship and generous heart. Daniel is still bragging about his 40th birthday! Truly over the top!

Chapter 6

Caesar's Palace in the distance, Las Vegas, USA.

A visit to Vegas always produces the same effect on us: who could dream of such exaggeration and opulence in the middle of a desert? But someone did have that vision, came up with a plan and tried to convince others it was a great place for casinos. Some investors were willing to take the risk. If you are paying down your home mortgage, you can leverage funds against the value of your property to invest again, and build your mini-Vegas. The Smith Manoeuvre is nothing like risking money playing roulette, however!

What Is Equity?

If you have paid down a substantial amount of your home mortgage, you have equity. Home equity is your portion of the value of your home. We say "your portion" because your lender has claim to the portion you haven't paid for yet. Equity does not pertain only to your home – the concept also applies to other valuables you own. We'll be talking about home equity, though, because most people build equity in their property. Home equity is an asset you can use to your advantage, so it is important to understand it.

Most of us need a mortgage or other loan to purchase a home. Let's assume you purchased your home for $200,000 and made a 20% down payment ($40,000); you borrow the remaining $160,000. Your equity in the home at this point is 20% of its value – that is, the $40,000 you have already paid. So you may say you own a home, but you really own only 20% of it. You can figure out how much home equity you have at any point by subtracting any money you owe on it from the home's current value.

Now let's look at the loan-to-value ratio. In metropolitan areas such as Vancouver and Toronto, the value of many homes doubled between 2000 and 2010. Let's assume you purchased a home for $200,000 and 10 years later it is worth $400,000. Let's say you still owe $160,000 on your mortgage. However, you now have 60% equity in your home. ($400,000 – $160,000 = $240,000, which is 60% of $400,000). The amount of your loan didn't change but your home equity increased because the value of the house increased as a result of real estate market conditions.

Every time you make a mortgage payment on your home loan, your equity increases. Every payment reduces the principal balance by a small amount and the rest of the payment covers interest. This slowly but surely reduces your loan and over time, a greater proportion from each payment goes toward the principal balance. In the sample payment summary below for a $350,000 mortgage with monthly payments of $1,701.58, notice that the portion of the payment going toward the principal increases slightly each month.

Payment date	Interest	Principal	Balance
Mar. 1, 2014	$941.56	$760.02	$349,239.98
Apr. 1, 2014	$939.52	$762.06	$348,477.92
May 1, 2014	$937.47	$764.11	$347,713.81
June 1, 2014	$935.41	$766.17	$346,947.64

We want you to be aware that the outcome is the opposite if real estate prices drop dramatically: you could be left owing the bank more on your mortgage than the house is worth – a very bad situation in which the bank will re-assess the home's value at the end of your term agreement, expecting you to pay the difference between the value and what you owe on the mortgage. This phenomenon caused many people in the United States to lose their homes during the recession beginning in 2008 because they could not pay the difference. The bank foreclosed on the mortgage and evicted home owners from their properties.

A colleague of ours is pursuing his own goals and hoping to retire soon. He built his own home and bought and sold many houses in a short time, hoping to build up profit. Although it is possible to make money by flipping homes, it's hard to come out on the winning side of this equation because of the expenses weighing down your profit every time you sell or buy: mortgage interest, real estate agent fees, lawyers' fees, land transfer tax, CMHC mortgage insurance and more. Furthermore, if the house you are selling is not your primary residence, you have to pay capital gains tax on any profit you make. We encourage people to hold onto their investment property longer to build equity and then use that equity as leverage: borrow from the bank against it and invest again. By having equity built up in your home you can now turn your mortgage into a tax-deductible investment expense using the Smith Manoeuvre (see below).

Chapter 6

Why Is Home Equity So Important?

Equity is an asset, a part of your total net worth. You can leverage it by borrowing against the value of your home or you can save it for future needs. You can borrow against it to invest in a second or third home, in dividend-paying stocks, in second mortgages or in any other investment vehicle. You can use it to pay off high-interest loans or to help pay for your children's education. It's an important asset, so choose your investments wisely; we'll talk more about that in Chapter 9. To do all this, you just need to set up a HELOC. Just remember that when you use your line of credit, you do pay interest on it, so be careful: make sure it's good debt. Also be sure that any investments you choose earn more than the interest you pay on your line of credit!

Some people confuse home equity lines of credit and second mortgages. Your home is used as collateral for both a HELOC and a second mortgage; both are loans against your home, so what's the difference? It's the way these loans are set up and paid out by the bank that's different. A HELOC is a revolving line of credit – in other words, your bank opens a line of credit account against the equity of your home, which guarantees the loan, protecting the bank in allowing you a line of credit. You can now borrow up to a maximum amount, and you make your monthly payments like you would for any loan. The payments are determined by the amount you owe, however, not by an agreement made when the loan is set up. Once you have paid off the borrowed money, you can borrow again without applying for another loan.

A second mortgage is a little different: your home is the collateral but the payout is set up differently. The loan is made to you in one lump sum. The amount is agreed upon, a setup fee is paid at the beginning and the terms and length of time to pay the loan back are established. Once the loan is paid off or you come to the end of the term agreement, you will need to reapply for a new loan, whereas a line of credit remains at your disposal as long as you make the required minimum payments. Remember that your home serves as collateral for both types of loans. If you can't make your payments, you risk losing your home and damaging your credit rating.

Harnessing the Power: The Smith Manoeuvre

If you live in the United States, you are lucky in the sense that the interest you pay on your mortgage is tax deductible. As Canadians, however, we cannot deduct the interest we pay. Fortunately, there is the Smith Manoeuvre. This powerful tool is one of the reasons we were able to retire early and join the fortunate few.

The Smith Manoeuvre, developed by Fraser Smith, is a way of making your assets work for you by essentially turning your largest non-deductible debt, your mortgage, into a tax-deductible investment loan. The technique is to borrow against your home equity and use the borrowed funds to invest in income-yielding products. This technique will increase your annual tax refund and take years off your mortgage loan if properly applied.

In Canada, it is legal to borrow money to invest in an income-producing venture, such as lending a second mortgage investment, buying dividend-paying stocks or buying rental real estate. The annual interest you pay on such an investment loan is deductible on your income tax return. You then put your increased tax refund toward your mortgage. Continue using the manoeuvre until your mortgage is paid off. Piece of cake!

One caveat: some are tempted to use their line of credit or to get a loan to contribute toward their RRSP. Be aware that you cannot deduct the interest paid on loans for contributions toward your RRSP investments. You need to analyze the tax benefit in your circumstance. Paying interest might be a small inconvenience considering the tax benefit you may get; however, this will depend on your marginal tax rate. In most cases, we suggest not borrowing to contribute to your RRSP because it defeats the purpose of deducting your interest charges.

Chapter 6

Here are the steps to turn an ordinary non-tax-deductible mortgage into a tax-deductible investment expense:

1. Open one of the combined mortgage/line of credit (HELOC) accounts we discussed in Chapter 5; we use National Bank of Canada's All-In-One account. Make your normal monthly mortgage payments from this account.

2. Use the assets you already have. For example, if your mortgage loan is $150,000 but your home is worth $500,000, you can use 80% of the $500,000 total, minus your mortgage loan. This means you qualify for a line of credit in the amount of $250,000. Here's how you calculate it: total value of your home × 80% − mortgage amount owing. In this example, that's $500,000 × .80 = $400,000 − $150,000 = $250,000. You may also want to consider selling any non-registered investments − that is, held outside your RRSPs − and depositing the proceeds in your HELOC to increase the amount available for buying investments.

3. With this HELOC account, you can now withdraw funds to invest in income-yielding products such as second mortgages, as we do, dividend-paying stocks, exchange-traded funds (ETFs) or rental real estate. With a HELOC, your credit limit increases and your mortgage principal decreases with every deposit you make, and thus the funds available for investment will increase whenever money goes into that account. Make sure you choose investments that yield a rate of return higher than the interest you pay on the borrowed funds. So if you pay 3.5% on your line of credit, make sure your investments provide returns above and beyond that 3.5%. We aim for 8% or more.

4. Every year when you complete your tax return, claim the interest you paid on your HELOC as a deductible expense. It is deductible because you used the borrowed funds to purchase income-producing investments. This is the piece of the manoeuvre that essentially turns your mortgage into a tax-deductible debt.

5. Next, place your income tax refund, plus any other revenue such as rental income, stock dividends or other investment or employment income, in your HELOC to reduce your non-deductible mortgage loan and increase the amount available in your credit line. Invest this available money and again deduct the interest you pay on that loan on your next tax return. So now you are making money (investment income) with funds you could not access without using this technique.

6. Continue Steps 3 to 5 of this process until your mortgage is paid off. With this system in place, you will be able to live off this income as we are and enjoy life among the fortunate few.

Some people have a hard time feeling comfortable with the Smith Manoeuvre because when they look at their *overall* debt, it never seems to decrease. This is because with this technique you keep borrowing against your home equity to invest, thus you don't reduce your overall debt. But if you use the manoeuvre properly and methodically, you can pay off your 25-year mortgage in as little as 17 years – or less – and build your investment portfolio at the same time. Once your mortgage is paid off in full, you can continue to use the manoeuvre to generate income. Rather than putting the profit toward your mortgage, you use it as income. Just remember that income is taxable.

The benefits

The Smith Manoeuvre has many benefits. For starters, your net worth will increase, assuming you can maintain rates of return on your investments that are higher than your borrowing rate. Your tax refunds will get larger (or your tax payable lower) year after year because the interest on your investment loan is tax deductible. Mortgage debt is a fact of life for most of us, so why not apply the Smith Manoeuvre, pay your mortgage off faster and transfer that debt to a tax-deductible expense?

The risks

The Smith Manoeuvre is a great tool, but it's not for everyone. Consult a licensed financial and tax advisor and/or an accountant, especially if you don't fully understand the procedure, before you embark on the manoeuvre. An independent financial advisor should communicate with your mortgage broker to help you make the best decisions and tailor the plan to your needs and comfort level.

As with any investment, there are risks. The Smith Manoeuvre doesn't reduce your debt, it transfers it from a mortgage, which isn't tax deductible in Canada, to tax-deductible investment debt. One significant risk is that the value of your house – the collateral for your investment loan – could fall below your borrowing power. Another risk is the ability of your investments to generate a rate of return that exceeds the rate you pay for borrowing in your line of credit. If they don't, you will be losing money.

Is it right for you?

You should not consider using the Smith Manoeuvre until you have *at least* 25% of your mortgage paid off, at which point you should qualify for a re-advanceable mortgage such as a line of credit or a second mortgage. You must be comfortable servicing "good" debt, you must be motivated to maximize your tax refund and you need to understand leveraging your real estate assets to increase your net worth.

If you're the type of person who likes to put things in place and then forget about them, the Smith Manoeuvre is not for you. This process requires clear planning and some effort on your part. You will need to select appropriate investments. You will need to check your accounts regularly and make sure your investments are performing and that your returns are above your borrowing rate. You and your accountant will have to carefully track use of funds (investment vs. personal) to ensure you deduct the correct amount at tax time.

If this technique is something you are interested in, we suggest you read Fraser Smith's book *The Smith Manoeuvre: Is Your Mortgage Tax Deductible*. Educate yourself and then talk with your accountant or financial advisor to find out if this is a good wealth-building strategy for you in your particular situation. It may seem complex at first but once you know how it works, you should become more comfortable with it.

Let's say you start with a mortgage of $300,000. Using the Smith Manoeuvre, the debt secured by your home equity stays the same at $300,000 but your mortgage gets paid off much faster than it normally would (because you are putting your bigger tax refunds toward it). If you borrow from your line of credit to invest in a second mortgage yielding, say, 8.5% to 12%, and therefore are able to pay off your mortgage in half the normal time, you still have a loan debt of $300,000 in your line of credit, but your investment is generating between $2,125 and $3,000 monthly. If you instead prefer to be debt-free, when the second mortgage investment contract comes to term, do not renew it; if it's another type of investment, sell it. Allow your investments to pay you back the full amount you have borrowed, and you will be debt-free.

Chapter 6

A Few Fortunate Thoughts about Equity

- Turn your equity into a powerful investment tool.

- Hold onto your investment property long enough to build equity and then use that as leverage: borrow against it and invest again. By having equity in your home you can turn your mortgage into a tax-deductible investment expense using the Smith Manoeuvre.

- Ensure that your investments earn you more than the interest you pay on your line of credit if this is where your investment money is coming from.

- Educate yourself and talk with your accountant and/or financial advisor to make informed wealth-building decisions.

- Use tools such as the Smith Manoeuvre and others not covered in this book. Learn the tricks of the trade and become an investment guru using what you have at your disposal. Be creative. You could be sitting on a gold mine without even knowing it.

Chapter 7
Budgeting

A budget is telling your money where to go instead of wondering where it went.

Dave Ramsey

Budgeting

Cliff hanger, Mont-Tremblant, Quebec

We decided to visit an aunt and her family in Mont-Tremblant, Quebec. Not only had we not seen these relatives in years but we also wanted to discover this wonderful area. Mont-Tremblant is a town in the Laurentian Mountains, halfway between Montreal and Ottawa; the area also features Mont-Tremblant National Park.

We visited in July and decided to try something new: mountain climbing. We ventured into the sport on a rock wall called La Vache noire (Black Cow). We discovered the Via Ferrata Mont-Tremblant, or "iron roads" – metal spikes protruding from the rock face. Clipped onto a steel cable that ran the length of the cliff, we crossed a challenging face with built-in steps, handles, beams and various types of bridges overlooking the meandering Diable River far below. Some climbers had to turn back when fear overwhelmed them. This is a sport that tests your ability to overcome your fears and exceed your comfort zone. As in the real world, people must venture out of their comfort zones, learn new skills, start a business, whatever. After making a 200-metre ascent, we were rewarded with a spectacular view of the mountains and horizon.

After our climbing excursion we arrived at Daniel's aunt's log home, with its soaring cathedral ceilings and large stone fireplace, perfect for romantic evenings. Peeking through a large sliding glass door, we could see an inviting hot tub on the patio. Our hosts were kind enough to suggest we relax there with a glass of wine while they started dinner. What an enjoyable way to recuperate after a strenuous day filled with a range of emotions. We were exhausted. Rock climbing was something we had always wanted to do; we could now check it off our bucket list.

Chapter 7

Carole on La Vache noire, Mont-Tremblant, Canada.

As we walked along the edge of the mountain, tied to a rope, taking one step at a time as our adrenaline was pumping through our veins, we felt the rush of overcoming fear and leaving our comfort zone! What if the rope snaps? What if the rod beneath our feet gives out? We persevered with determination. We looked forward, keeping our focus. We were rewarded with a spectacular view. Budgeting money is a bit like that – you may wonder if it's worth the sacrifices along the way, but remember that financial freedom is priceless! Start paying yourself now!

Saving Is Part of Budgeting

People often believe there's no way they can save. But in reality there are simple practices you can apply that can help. We stopped counting the books and seminars that insisted on the same principle: "Pay yourself first!" That may sound either impossible or overly simplistic, but it's true.

Paying yourself first is a key to financial freedom and we suggest you do this by opening a savings account and setting up automatic withdrawals from your chequing account monthly. Pay yourself 10% of every paycheque. Consider having your employer automate a withdrawal from your pay to put toward your RRSP if you feel you don't have the discipline. You will find that by setting money aside this way, you won't miss it.

Single annual income	10% per year	Two-income family
$30,000	$3,000	$6,000
40,000	4,000	8,000
60,000	6,000	12,000
80,000	8,000	16,000
100,000	10,000	20,000

In concrete terms, the question is, could you and your partner survive with $19 less per day? Some may say no, but if your annual household net income is $70,000 (according to Statistics Canada, in 2011 the Canadian average was just under $80,000) and you save 10%, $19 a day – just $133 each week – is all we're talking about. Both our fathers said it: "It's not how much you make, it's how much you save." The trick to building wealth is investing and to invest, you first need to save.

Look at the table above and estimate how long it will take you to save the 20% down payment you'll need to purchase your first, second or third home. If you follow the 10% saving guideline, with your $70,000 household income, you and your partner will accumulate $35,000 in as little as five years and $70,000 in 10 years. If you invest in some of the diversified vehicles we use, including real estate, and earn 8% to 12%, you are well on your way to becoming financially independent and joining the fortunate few. If you are able to save even just $5,000 each year for 40 years, and invest it at 8%, at the end of those 40 years you will have accumulated $1.3 million.

We are in our 40s and are living the same lifestyle as when we were working full time. Actually, not quite – our lifestyle now includes being free from alarm clocks, free from full-time employment and free from having a boss. We can do what we want with our time and this is precious to us. But financially speaking, we live as if we had a steady income, the same way we did when working full time. We say this to impress upon you that it's completely realistic for you to be among the fortunate few and live this kind of free lifestyle by applying the techniques we're describing; saving is one of them. It is also critically important to be reasonable in your spending habits and to stay focused on your goal. Developing good habits, sticking to your plan and writing out your to-do lists will help you do that.

Also take into account that by the time we are 67, the government provides all Canadians with Old Age Security income. This program provides a modest income if you have lived in Canada for at least 10 years. If you are a low-income senior, you may be eligible for other benefits as early as age 60. These payments aren't enough to provide financial freedom, but don't forget to include them in your calculations. Investigate Service Canada's website to find out what you might qualify for: *http://www.servicecanada.gc.ca.*

How to Budget

Never spend more than your disposable income. That's another principle we consider to be a golden rule. It sounds painfully obvious, but it's the only way you can save money.

Chapter 7

Create a spreadsheet for your budget. Divide it into debit and credit categories. In your debit column, list all your expenses – and we mean *all*: this column should include your monthly mortgage payments; bills such as phones, electricity and water; all types of insurance; groceries; car payments and other costs; child or spousal support payments; your monthly 10% pay-yourself-first allocation; other loan payments, dance lessons; your children's sports registrations; cash for your daily latte fix – in short, any and all funds withdrawn from your account.

In your credit column, list all your sources of income: your pay or salary (net income), child or spousal support, rental or other investment income and any other money that comes in. Here's an example:

Download for Monthly Family Budget Worksheet available here: *http://www.thefortunatefew.com/tools-and-resources/*

Budgeting

Monthly family budget

	Description	Credit	Debit	Balance	Notes
Income	Paycheques	5,800			Net, both spouses
	Rental income	200			Net, after expenses
Total income				6,000	
Expenses	Mortgage		1,500		
	Savings		600		Pay yourself first: RRSP, RESP, TFSA
	Food		350		
	Car		800		Loan payment, insurance, fuel
	Home maintenance		200		
	Home insurance		200		
	Utilities		480		Gas, electricity, water
	Medical expenses		50		
	Clothing		50		
	Entertainment		200		Restaurant meals, movies, clubs
	Cable TV		60		
	Phones, Internet		200		
	Fitness membership		200		
	Kids' activities/lessons		400		
	Dance lessons		400		
	Miscellaneous		160		Magazine subscription, coffee shop
Total expenses				5,850	
Excess of income over expenses				150	Available for additional savings or emergencies

If you have a partner or spouse, fill in your spreadsheet together. If you have teenaged children, include them as well. Make this a team effort so you all clearly understand where your expenses are and what your income is. Start taking responsibility for your financial health and start budgeting. But keep it simple; do not get obsessed with it. Simply list your expenses and your income. This step alone will make you take action on reducing some expenses. If you discover expenses are greater than income, you need to budget to make them fit – and that's what most people have trouble with. Your monthly magazine subscriptions, for example, might be something you can live without – perhaps they're available online for free. Be careful not to give the budgeting exercise negative associations. Instead of thinking of the pain of cutting back, think of the pleasure of getting closer to achieving your goals.

Paying for Your Children's Education

One of the biggest expenses you may foresee for your middle years is your children's higher education. Of course most parents want to help their children. And most parents believe paying for their children's education is a key way of helping them. But is it? We'd like to get you thinking about that.

We have seen too many students and recent graduates slacking because things come too easily to them – their parents provide everything. We have always believed in teaching our son the value of money and we've done this by having him pay his own way. Even when we travelled to Europe for three weeks we gave Corey (16 years old at the time) money that had to last him three weeks. Needless to say, he ran out and had to borrow from us. Upon our return he had to pay us back. This was a great lesson for him.

A major part of being a good parent is teaching your children to be independent, and a big part of being independent is knowing how to manage money. Educate your children. Invest in them by teaching them every day and showing them the family's monthly financial obligations. Teach them to budget. Talk about the family finances. Have them write out the cheque or complete the online transfer to pay a bill next time you need to. Show them all your household bills. Have your kids do things like pay the cashier when you go to the supermarket together. This not only makes them realize how much groceries cost but also teaches them to interact with the cashier and count money. Do the same thing when filling your car with gas.

The arrangement we had with our son was that we would pay for his last year of higher education. Knowing from an early age that this was the deal, he started to save while in high school, working part time. He successfully saved enough money for his first year of university. He enrolled in a five-year co-op program that allowed him to not only gain work experience but also finance his program on his own.

It's tough love!

You might be wondering what will become of the education fund you've put aside for your kids if you decide not to pay for the full cost of their post-secondary education. Whenever you talk with your children about what they want in terms of education and a profession, explain to them that it is important for them to plan their budget because they will have to pay for most of their education. Explain that the education fund will assist them with their final year of education, if that's what you decide. We elaborate more on how RESP contributions work in Chapter 8. This will instill in them a commitment to and accountability for their own success and make them understand the financial implications of their decisions. The day they truly understand that they are responsible for paying for their own education will be the day they commit to securing employment. This in itself is a great life lesson.

Helping your children purchase their first home is of far greater help to them than paying for post-secondary education. If your children have learned the value of money by this time, which they should have if they have already worked for 10 years and paid for most of

Chapter 7

their own education, they will appreciate help with a home all the more.

Education is obviously very important; all we are saying is that children should take charge of their own success, learn the value of money and learn that investing in themselves brings rewards.

We encourage budgeting money to help your children – but think hard about what that money will be for.

Let your children fend for themselves. They will learn to make better decisions if you don't do everything for them and provide everything for them. As parents, our responsibility is instead to make our children independent and give them the confidence and the tools they need to succeed.

Buying them a car, paying for their education and paying their monthly smartphone bill is not doing them any favours – in fact, you are slowly setting them up for failure and hardship in the future. Instead, teach them what they need to know to make it out there on their own. Start teaching them basic budgeting when they are very young.

Carole's father is a very wise man. He and his wife raised five daughters and a son. We have sat with him on many occasions to chat about how their values shaped their children into the individuals they are today. All are successful and none ever got into trouble – that we are aware of! After a few discussions with them, we believe they are experts and we witness the proof at each family gathering. Among the many things they taught us is the French expression, *qu'ils s'arrangent!* It means let them figure it out! This is a valuable lesson. Children are too protected and sometimes, we do too much for them.

A Few Fortunate Thoughts on Budgeting

- Start saving with a simple, realistic principle: pay yourself 10% of your household income. Saving money might seem impossible for some. It's easier if you automate that withdrawal from your pay and have the money deposited in a separate account or directly to your RRSP.

- Keep a regular check on your spending habits, individually and as a family, and balance your budget. Make the family finances a shared responsibility. If you have children who are old enough to participate, involving them is the best way to teach them. Spend within your means – this is the golden rule to budgeting and it helps with credit card spending and reaching your goals.

- Make your children independent and give them the confidence and the tools to succeed. As parents, that's our responsibility. Let your children fend for themselves; they will learn to make better decisions.

Chapter 8
Saving

If you cannot do great things, do small things in a great way.
Napoleon Hill

Saving

Paradise in the Borinquen Mountains, Costa Rica

Daniel

For Carole's birthday, I took her to the Borinquen Mountain Resort and Spa at Rincón de la Vieja Volcano. The resort and hot springs is an exclusive vacation spot located in the province of Guanacaste in the North Pacific Region of Costa Rica, where we own a home.

The Anáhuac Spa at Borinquen offers a unique natural setting – the name Anáhuac comes from the local native language and means "surrounded by water." The Zen-inspired building is in the forest, right over a sparkling stream and close to a volcanic vent. A more enchanting site is hard to imagine! We envisioned breakfast in bed and romantic candlelight dinners. We couldn't wait to get there.

We packed our things, got on our motorbike and took to the winding roads. When we arrived at the breathtakingly beautiful resort, perched on a mountainside, we walked up a path through manicured gardens to find our villa. It was truly amazing. We kissed like newlyweds.

We freshened up and made our way to the thermal baths. There was no one in sight; it was low season so we had the whole place to ourselves! We visited the unique sauna first – it was a cabin sitting over natural boiling mud pools. The steam from these fumaroles made its way through the crevices in the wooden floor to heat the sauna. The whole thing was just amazing!

When we left the sauna, we found an urn of hot volcanic mud in the spa. I led Carole by the hand and then sunk my hands into the warm, soothing clay. "Are you ready?" I asked. She looked at me with an inviting smile and nodded. I scooped up mud and carefully spread the warm paste on her body, using nothing but my hands. I made sure I covered every inch of her body, delicately adding a final touch to her face before whispering, "I'm done" in her ear.

She leaned over to kiss me and we began to laugh – I now had mud all over my face. She then plunged her hands into the mud, announcing, "Your turn, mon amour!"

After this sensuous experience, we showered the mud off. Our skin was silky soft. We headed to the thermal bath, amazed at this hot water coming from the depths of the earth. We spent several hours in the bath, with no one in sight, wine in hand, listening to the birds and howler monkeys in the distance and letting our bodies be infused with the healing properties of the water.

Chapter 8

We finished the evening with a romantic dinner and made our way back to our villa, walking in the moonlight, millions of stars glowing above us. What a spectacular day.

Playing in the mud, Borinquen Mountains, Costa Rica.

Saving

We all have our best birthday moments engraved in our memories and marking time is important, even if we need to admit we are growing older. Taking care of your health is the best way to ensure a good quality of life. We believe another great thing you can do for yourself is knowing how to save to be able to enjoy life. As Canadians, we have many savings vehicles at our disposal, as you can see below.

Just as we sometimes need to revitalize and renew our bodies and souls, we must also sometime take a step back and rethink and refresh our finances.

Chapter 8

Registered Retirement Savings Plans

RRSPs, created by the government to encourage people to save for retirement, are a great Canadian savings and investment vehicle that you must not ignore. An RRSP is just a container: it can hold savings accounts, guaranteed investment certificates (GICs), mutual funds, individual stocks, bonds, mortgage loans, income trusts, foreign currency and labour-sponsored funds.

What is an RRSP?

Most Canadians know basically what an RRSP is – most will say, "It's that investment we contribute to every year for our retirement and to get a tax refund." But an RRSP is much more than that and requires more than yearly contributions for optimal growth. You have decisions to make: an effective RRSP is not just a savings account or a mutual fund and isn't there just to generate tax refunds.

When you contribute to your RRSP at a bank, the bank will often sell you one of its mutual fund packages. Many people with RRSPs never consider investing in other vehicles, such as mortgage investment corporations. They simply contribute for tax benefits and then leave it there, seeing it as their pension plan. That's fine, but your RRSP can generate much more for you. The major benefit of RRSPs is that any earnings (interest, investment gains, etc.) in it are sheltered from tax until the funds are withdrawn. The idea is that when you retire and begin using the money, you will be in a lower tax bracket and therefore pay less tax on the money than you would have when you earned it. Because you can claim RRSP contributions as income tax deductions, they help to reduce income taxes paid now if you are a high-income earner.

It's really important to start saving in your RRSP or TFSA as soon as you start earning income. There is no minimum age requirement for RRSPs, so even teens with part-time jobs should be encouraged to open plans. See Rules for RRSPs, below, for information on contribution limits.

Starting early is critical because the longer your contributions stay invested, the more money they will earn for you – you'll be earning interest on your interest. For example, if you would like to have $1 million available in your RRSP when you turn 65, if you start investing at age 25 you will need to contribute about $7,900 per year to your RRSP, earning 5% interest. If you wait until you are 45 to get started, you will need to contribute more than three times more each year – about $29,000 – to earn that million.

You are allowed to contribute up to 18% of your annual income to your RRSP. If you are able to make yearly RRSP contributions of $10,000, you will enjoy a tax refund or tax reduction of approximately $4,500 if you are in the top tax bracket. If you can afford to contribute $10,000 to your RRSP every year for 10 years, you will have invested $100,000 and received tax refunds or reductions amounting to approximately $45,000. The Canada Revenue Agency (CRA) allows you to withdraw up to $11,000 a year from your RRSP tax free if you have no other source of income. This amount may fluctuate slightly from year to year but it is set by the CRA and represents the amount of income someone can earn without having to pay taxes. If you are able to accumulate $200,000 in your RRSP portfolio, you can withdraw $11,000 a year for 18 years, with no taxes to pay if you don't have other income.

If you are not able to contribute the full 18% in a given year, the unused portion can be carried over to following years.

Investing in RRSPs shouldn't simply be about tax refunds and basic savings. You need to invest your contributions in vehicles such as bonds, individual stocks, mutual funds and yes, even mortgages that will really work for you and earn significant interest, rather than leaving it in a savings account earning 2%.

Some people are lucky enough to have generous employer pensions they can rely on as their sole retirement income (of course the feasibility of this depends on the size of your pension and the type of lifestyle you desire). If you have a good company pension, you won't have to contribute as much to you RRSP. If you're in this situation, you may want to consider investing in a TFSA instead, though you should not ignore the tax-deferral benefits of RRSPs.

But if you, like most people, do not have a good pension plan at work, or any pension at all, you should contribute your yearly maximum of 18% of your total income to an RRSP.

Investing in your RRSP

People have different levels of comfort with risk, and your risk tolerance will be a big part of determining how you invest your RRSP. Your goal is for your portfolio to continue to grow. However, most of us have seen the value of our investments decline since 2008. Some believe a good place to start with your RRSP is with a reputable mutual fund. We use our RRSP for higher-risk investments because we also have some lower-risk investments, such as real estate, outside our RRSPs.

Your best protection against volatility is to diversify across different types of investments (such as mutual funds, bonds and individual stocks) and to know what kind of investor you are and what you are comfortable with. Many experts believe that ETFs are useful and they generally have lower fees and greater growth potential. People who have a lot of money to invest will have both registered (RRSP) and non-registered portfolios. Non-registered accounts do not have contribution limits and any earnings on them are taxed in the year they are earned; contributions are not tax deductible. If you have both registered and non-registered portfolios, you might invest in higher-earning vehicles (income trusts and MICs, for example) inside your RRSP. Capital gains and dividends on stocks are taxed at a lower rate than interest income, so these might be better outside your RRSP. Talk to your own financial advisor about what makes sense in your particular situation.

Do your homework – learn about investing. Don't rely solely on your bank representative's guidance. Investigate the fees attached to different types of investments. Consider the best asset allocation for you; that is, what portion of your investments you want in higher-risk growth vehicles and what portion should be in safer investments. If you don't invest wisely, you could end up with a loss. You need to be disciplined, educated and informed. Managing your investments is like holding a part-time job. In our opinion, you are best off sticking to proven strategies and diversifying your investments. Although mutual funds are the most popular investment for retirement, and they are a good choice if you're just starting out, investigate what else is out there.

If you are leery of investing because your RRSP portfolios are smaller than they were five or 10 years ago, we understand. For most investments, the years since 2008 have been characterized by great volatility and performance has been very difficult to predict. In the long run, however, you will see that your investments will bounce back. For example, a couple who started investing $10,000 yearly at age 35 at a rate equivalent to that of the S&P/TSX Composite Index and are now 65 would have $400,000 because of constant contributions and growth over the past 30 years, despite the fluctuations in the Index.

In the end, regardless of your investments' performance, you still benefited from the tax breaks when you made those RRSP contributions. Remember that this investment is for retirement, for the long term. Watch for opportunities and stay on track by investing carefully.

If you read Chapter 3, Time Management and Planning, you should have a good idea how to stay focused and make sure you are on the right path to attain your objectives. Many people skip RRSP contributions in the early part of their careers – and this seems natural; they're focusing on career improvement, mortgage, family and paying off debts. But if you follow our recommendations on planning and budgeting, RRSP contributions will be part of your plan and your budget and you will be on track.

Let's say you and your spouse want to accumulate a total of half a million dollars in your RRSPs. Compound interest calculators are available online that will show you how much you should contribute and when you should start. If you start in your late 20s and put in $10,000 ($5,000 each) every year for 25 years, assuming a 5% annual interest rate, you will reach your $500,000 goal. Many people find that they actually surpass their goals.

Generally, you should change your RRSP investment strategy as you get older, unless you are already investing in lower-risk strategies. As you get closer to retirement, your portfolio should be more conservative; that is, you will need to change your asset allocation. When you are younger, in your 20s to early 40s, it's fine to have 50% to 60% of your savings in high-risk investments such as equities (shares). If your investments take a turn for the worse, you still have time to recover. But once you are in your late 40s and beyond, your funds need to be invested in safer, low-risk vehicles.

A general rule of thumb for asset allocation is to subtract your age from 80; the result is the percentage you should invest in stocks or other higher-risk investments. So if you're 30, you can feel comfortable investing 50% of your portfolio in stocks. If you are 50, you should probably invest only 30% in stocks. This depends on your individual situation, so discuss it with your investment advisor.

When you are no longer working, you stop making RRSP contributions and you can start to withdraw from your RRSP account. Many will point out that after you have benefited from tax deferral all those years you contributed to your plan, the government is now waiting on the sidelines to collect. This is partially correct: if you pull out $100,000 a year from your RRSP, you will be taxed as if it were income – in the 43% tax bracket, so you would pay approximately $43,000 in tax, leaving you with only $57,000.

However, if your finances permit, you could withdraw $11,000 a year and pay no tax if you have no other income. If you and your spouse both do this, you can withdraw $22,000 each year, tax free. Remember that by this stage in your life, if you planned well, you will have no mortgage on your principal home, no car payments and no bad debt. You might own only one car (paid off), thus saving on auto expenses. Therefore, $22,000 is a substantial amount when it isn't taxed. This doesn't mean you can't withdraw more. You can withdraw $40,000 each and pay as little as $5,861 in taxes (because you will not be in the top tax bracket). Calculate which tax bracket you will be in when considering how much to withdraw – the government will want its share of your gains.

Spousal RRSPs

A spousal RRSP is one that is in the name of and controlled by one spouse but to which the other, higher-income spouse makes contributions under their own contribution limit (and receives the tax deduction).

Spousal contributions are useful if one spouse is making significantly more income than the other – they are a way of splitting, or balancing, income to help ensure that both spouses have approximately the same income at retirement, which can save income tax.

If you or your spouse has a pension, you will need to consider it in conjunction with spousal RRSP plans. Spouses receiving pension income can now move up to 50% of this income from their own plan to their spouse's plan, minimizing income taxes they pay because it shifts the higher-earning spouse's income to the lower-income spouse. You will now receive two smaller incomes at retirement, taxed at a lower rate, rather than having one spouse receiving a large income in a higher tax bracket.

Here's an example: If you are earning $60,000 in pension income and your spouse earns no income, you would pay approximately $15,000 in federal and provincial income tax. By splitting that income between the two of you ($30,000 each), you would pay a *total* of approximately $10,000 because of the change in tax brackets – a tax saving of approximately $5,000 every year, depending on what province you live in.

Income splitting applies only to people 65 or older, but we think it's important to be aware of this approach so that you can plan ahead.

Chapter 8

Rules for RRSPs

Contribution limits

The CRA calculates how much you can contribute for the upcoming year based on your current year's earnings and communicates the amount with your Income Tax Assessment after you file your taxes. You can contribute up to 18% of your income; however, the government also sets a maximum dollar contribution every year ($24,270 for the 2014 tax year). You can find information on limits on the CRA website: *http://www.cra-arc.gc.ca/tx/rgstrd/papspapar-fefespfer/lmts-eng.html*. If you did not contribute the maximum you were allowed in previous years, unused contribution room rolls over into the next year. If you contribute too much, the excess will be carried forward for your next year's contribution and you won't receive the tax break until the following year. As well, CRA may charge you interest and possibly a penalty on the over-contribution, so stay within the limit.

The allowable contribution to a spousal RRSP depends on the *contributor's* available contribution room.

Home Buyers Plan

You are allowed to borrow up to $25,000 from your own RRSP to use as a down payment toward the purchase of your first home under the federal Home Buyers Plan. We say borrow because you must repay that amount to your RRSP within 15 years. This can work well because you don't pay taxes or interest on the borrowed money. Note that your RRSP growth will be affected because there is $25,000 less in the account.

You can do the same for your education. You can withdraw $20,000 from your RRSPs tax free to finance full-time studies (a maximum of $10,000 per year; you can do this twice). As with the Home Buyers Plan, you must repay this amount within 15 years.

If you withdraw money from your RRSP for anything else, you will pay income tax on that money according to your income level. You

Saving

can learn more about the Home Buyers Plan here: *http://www.cra-arc. gc.ca/tx/ndvdls/tpcs/rrsp-reer/menu-eng.html*.

Conversion to a Registered Retirement Income Fund

You are not permitted to contribute to your RRSP after you turn 71. Once you're 71, you must either withdraw the money, purchase an annuity or convert the RRSP to a RRIF. You must then withdraw a minimum amount each year. You will receive a notice from your financial institution informing you of the minimum amount you are required to withdraw. On average, you will be required to withdraw somewhere between 6% and 8% per year; this amount will increase to around 20% as you get closer to your 90s.

We suggest that you plan to have less than $506,000 in your RRSP when you reach 71. Plan to use your RRSP to enjoy life while you are still healthy and able. By the time you are 71 you will be receiving government income, including Canada Pension, Old Age Security and possibly the Guaranteed Income Supplement, and that money, in addition to the remainder of your RRSP (which will be transferred to a RRIF), will enable you to live comfortably. If you use up your RRSPs early, as we did, and have other investments such as real estate, you may be able to live comfortably off rental income.

Taxation and RRSPs

You can find information on income tax rates on the CRA's website, at *http://www.cra-arc.gc.ca/tx/ndvdls/fq/txrts-eng.html*. In Canada we have both federal and provincial income taxes, and deductions and credits vary according to province. Tax rates also differ depending on your province and income level.

We want to reinforce that whenever you withdraw money from your RRSP, you will be taxed on that amount according to your income level. Also note that investing in an RRSP is one of the very few ways you can avoid paying capital gains tax when you sell the investment and avoid paying tax on interest and dividends as you earn them.

Understanding how marginal tax rates apply to your salary is very important because it helps you understand your net income. Gross income is the money you have before you pay your taxes. If you are planning your finances or budgeting for retirement, the focus should be on your net income.

In conclusion

The beauty of RRSPs is compound interest growth and the fact that your tax payment is deferred. Deferred tax is like a zero-interest loan from the government. You don't repay the loan until decades later, in retirement. There's a lot more to RRSPs than just making your yearly contributions and counting down till retirement. If you have made your contributions conscientiously and have been successful in investing in the right vehicles, you should be able to consider retiring earlier than you had planned. You will not need as much money when you are older because you will have no debt or at least less debt. This will allow you to live on much less, thus paying less tax on the money you withdraw from your RRSP. Plan to use up most of your RRSP before you turn 71 because at that point you will be forced to start withdrawing it.

We retired young and are withdrawing a little every year, staying in the low tax bracket. We plan on doing this until our RRSPs are used up. After that, we will rely on our real estate investments. By then, all our rental homes will be paid off, so we can decide whether we want to sell them or live off the rental income. Just remember that capital gains tax is payable when you sell a property other than your principal dwelling.

There are some great ways of taking advantage of the system to create tax breaks. Consult your accountant. One example is deferring your RRSP deductions to later years if you are in your early years of investing. Doing so allows you to use your tax break when you are in a higher tax bracket, thus helping you keep more of your money. Another example is investing in flow-through shares issued by certain mining and oil exploration companies. The tax credit savings you get from the government for investing with these firms can offset the taxes you pay on RRSP withdrawals. But be sure to discuss this with your accountant or investment advisor.

Tax-Free Savings Accounts

TFSAs were introduced by the federal government in 2009. They're another great investment vehicle that cannot be ignored. TFSAs should be used by those in lower income brackets, who can't benefit from the RRSPs tax deduction. That's not to say they're only for low-income earners – TFSAs can be a powerful tool for higher-income earners as well.

The maximum yearly contribution you can make to your TFSA increases occasionally. From 2009 to 2013 it was $5,000 and in 2014, it rose to $5,500. You must be at least 18 to open a TFSA, but they don't have upper age limits as RRSPs do. You can use your TFSA until your last breath: you will never be forced to withdraw from this account. You can contribute to your TFSA at any time. TFSA contributions are cumulative since 2009 for everyone who was 18 or older that year – the government allows you to catch up on any years you did not make your maximum contribution. For example, if you contribute $2,000 this year, rather than the $5,500 maximum, next year you can contribute $9,000 ($3,500 from this year plus $5,500 for next year). So you are never penalized for not being able to make your yearly maximum contribution. On top of that, any amount withdrawn from your TFSA is added back onto your contribution limit for the *following* year. Just be careful not to over-contribute in any given year or you could face a penalty. If you should pass away, your TFSA account is automatically part of your estate with no tax liability. There are different rules in some provinces so check local regulations.

Let's look at how much you can save in a TFSA:

Year	Age	Cumulative maximum contributions
1	18	$5,500 ($5,000 for 2009–13)
2	19	11,000
3	20	16,500
4	21	22,000
5	22	27,500
6	23	33,000
7	24	38,500
8	25	44,000

In eight short years you are allowed to contribute up to $44,000 to a TFSA. So a couple is able to contribute up to $88,000, with all interest earned tax free. In 16 years you and your partner can contribute up to $176,000. Let's say your goal is to retire at 40. You will have 22 years of contribution allowance in your name (from age 18 to 40), so for both partners combined that's $242,000. If you invest it properly, this can double to a whopping $454,000. Not bad for staying the course, with the added bonus of not paying taxes on investment gains.

Should I Invest in a TFSA or RRSP?

A TFSA is a way to shelter *earnings* on your savings from being taxed. An RRSP, on the other hand, gives you a tax break on the contributions you make. Any money you withdraw is taxed based on your income bracket for that year. You can't claim money invested in TFSAs to offset your income as you do with RRSPs.

If you earn less than about $40,000 per year, you may want to consider investing your savings in a TFSA. When you are in a lower income bracket you pay less tax and so generally don't need the tax breaks. If your annual income is higher than $40,000, you can invest in your TFSA but also contribute to your RRSP to take advantage of tax breaks.

Planning is important: you might look at an RRSP as a better long-term investment and reap the benefits in tax sheltering. However, you may be saving to buy an investment property and hope to have a 20% down payment in less than five years. In this case, investing in your TFSA may be a better strategy. Everyone's situation is different and only your planning strategy can determine the best investment vehicle to use. If you are fortunate and have ample funds available, we suggest you maximize your contributions to both your RRSP and TFSA. If you don't have enough to do both, you could make your maximum contribution to your RRSP and use the resulting tax refund to invest in your TFSA.

You will need to consider many factors when deciding where to invest. Some people prefer to save in TFSAs early in their careers because they need to be able to withdraw the funds to buy furniture, pay for the kids' lessons and so on without tax consequences. However, if you start contributing early enough to your RRSP, as we mentioned earlier, as a first-time home buyer you can withdraw up to $25,000 to put toward your down payment or $20,000 to invest in your education.

We think most young adults give precedence to investing in TFSAs rather than RRSPs for the simple reason that they are generally in a lower tax bracket at the beginning of their career. Again, talk with your accountant or financial advisor to assess what investment strategy best fits your circumstances. Most accountants will agree that later in your life, when you are making $80,000 or more, you are likely to want the tax relief offered by RRSPs.

Are TFSAs safer than RRSPs? Is your money secure? The answer is, it depends what you invest in. Like an RRSP, a TFSA is simply an account where you store your money. You have to decide how you should invest this money to capitalize on compound interest. Both types of accounts can hold safe but low-earning savings accounts or riskier but potentially higher-earning mutual funds and many other types of investments. What you choose depends on your investment profile, including your age and risk tolerance.

Registered Education Savings Plans

Unlike with RRSPs, contributions to RESPs are not tax deductible; however, you also avoid taxes on investment growth within the RESP. There is no annual limit for contributions to RESPs but there is a $50,000 lifetime limit on the amount that can be contributed for a single beneficiary.

When funds are withdrawn from an RESP, income tax must be paid on earnings. When funds are withdrawn and tax is paid, it is the *student* who must claim the income and pay the tax, not the contributor. Because the student will almost certainly be in a lower income bracket, the total tax paid will be much less than if the original contributor were the one to be taxed on the withdrawal.

What is unique about the RESP is that the federal government adds an annual Canadian Education Savings Grant to your contributions, matching up to 20% of the annual contribution, to a lifetime maximum of $7,200. When grant money is withdrawn from the RESP, the student must also declare this as income and pay any tax owing.

If your children choose not to pursue post-secondary education, instead of closing the account and getting taxed on the interest earned, consider transferring the funds to your RRSP if you have sufficient contribution room. You can transfer up to $50,000 of the contributions you made to the RESP into your RRSP. To qualify, the RESP must have been open for at least 10 years and all beneficiaries must be at least age 21. Note that the financial institution holding the plan will return the Canadian Education Savings Grants, along with interest on the grants, to the government if it is unused.

If you decide to cash out your RRSP, you won't be taxed on the amount you transferred from the RESP, but you will have to pay tax on the money you earned on the transferred funds, such as dividends and interest. An individual or family RESP can stay open for 36 years, so an alternative is to keep your RESP open. Your child, now an adult, may change his or her mind and go back to school later.

As with RRSPs and TFSAs, you can choose how you want to invest money from this account for positive results.

For more information on how RESPs are managed, see *http://www.cra-arc.gc.ca/tx/ndvdls/tpcs/rrsp-reer/rrsps-eng.html*.

A Few Fortunate Thoughts about Savings

- Set up pre-authorized payments to help you contribute to your RRSP or spousal RRSPs – they shelter your savings from tax while accumulating compound interest. Plan your withdrawals by calculating how much tax you are willing to pay.

- TFSAs are vehicles that allow you to grow your gains tax free and can be useful for low- and high-income earners. TFSAs are a powerful tool for those who thrive on high-yielding investments because profits are not taxed, even upon withdrawal.

- RESPs are a benefit because the government grants you 20% of your investment. Your child will have to claim that money as income – another good way to develop their awareness of taxes!

- Study the pros and cons of every contribution vehicle available before you choose. Study your 10-year plan and make your decisions accordingly. Consult a financial advisor and use your accountant to focus on a strategy that will benefit you. Understanding these investment vehicles is important – they must be part of your Life Planning Worksheet.

Chapter 9
Investing

You'll miss 100% of the shots you don't take.
Wayne Gretzky

The Iron Lady and the Queen of the Night, Paris, France

We left for France at the beginning of September to take part in a family reunion marking the arrival of our Drouin ancestors in Canada over 400 years ago. We were welcomed like royalty. The celebration was held in a castle on the outskirts of Paris in a small medieval village called Le Pin-La-Garenne. We could hear church bells ringing at a distance all around us. These bells reached faraway lands: distant cousins from all over the world gathered. This was an exceptional trip for Carole's parents and we love to reminisce together about how we were welcomed by our hosts and how the village was decorated for the event. It is hard to explain how completely this village made us feel welcomed and how they appreciated our presence.

We prolonged our stay in France to visit Paris, the city of lights and love. We spent an unforgettable weekend in the capital and still rave about our evening cruise on a bateau-mouche along the River Seine through the heart of Paris. We boarded at the foot of the Eiffel Tower and set sail as the sun set and the city lights flickered on. We had visited the Louvre Museum and the cruise was the perfect way to finish our day, sitting comfortably, taking everything in, slowly floating through enchanting neighbourhoods. During the cruise we discovered some of the most prestigious landmarks along the route, such as Notre Dame Cathedral, the Musée d'Orsay and Pont Neuf.

We cuddled up and admired some of the most celebrated Parisian monuments, their splendour enhanced by the lights as a soft accordion melody from the back of the boat resonated around us, gently echoing off walls and bridges as we glided along. The one and only Eiffel Tower was waiting for us at the end of our tour, tall and strong, proudly reflecting the colours of the French flag, transitioning from silver to red to blue. The tower pointed straight toward the heavens, where a full moon brightly shone like the queen of the night . Everything was so romantic and perfect. Magnifique! We stepped off the boat and walked slowly toward the Eiffel Tower, wanting that evening to last forever.

Chapter 9

Lovers and the Iron Lady, Paris, France.

We were lucky to travel to France, the country where our families are rooted, and to take part in the celebration of our ancestors' voyage to the le nouveau monde. They risked their lives hoping for a better future. We didn't have to risk our lives for a better life – we owe our success to real estate investments and we are comfortable with the level of risk involved. Read on to learn how we do it.

Chapter 9

Before You Start Investing...

Don't live beyond your means. Purchase big-ticket items only once all debts are paid off. Include major acquisitions in your 10-year plan to reduce impulse or gratification buying. Paying off debt should be your first investment choice. Once your high-interest debts are paid, start using the investment vehicles available to you, such as those described in Chapter 8.

Financial education is important – the more you understand, the more skilled and successful you will be. First, you need to appreciate the difference between higher-risk and lower-risk investment and what diversifying an investment portfolio means. We will focus on the investment strategies we use or tried ourselves and demonstrate how they brought us to where we are today.

In this chapter we will talk about ways you can invest the funds you contribute to your RRSP and TFSA – the investments in these accounts can be high or low risk. We will review investment properties and how real estate remains a good asset for us, even in today's economy. We will also discuss investing in first and second mortgages and finally we will look at the stock market.

Diversifying

As an investor, you need to assess your level of comfort with risk – it's different for everyone. For us, diversification is an important part of our strategy to mitigate risk. Risk refers to how "safe" your money is in the investment. With high-risk investments you could lose everything. But they can also be highly successful and earn you more money. Low-risk investments are safer – you are unlikely to lose all your money – but generally earn lower returns too.

If you invest in something that has a good track record, such as bank stocks, you are lessening your risk. If you invest in mining companies, and your success depends on mineral test results in a given area, this is a higher-risk investment because it's not a sure thing. If you invest in mining knowing there's definitely gold to be extracted, the risk is lowered because you are basing your investment on facts. Investing in a company that has never yielded its projected return on investment would be considered high risk. If you were told that your investment had a 50/50 chance of producing your expected return, it would be considered high risk. Investing in something you know nothing about is high risk. At the other end of the spectrum, Canada Savings Bonds present almost no risk to investors, but your return is lower in most cases.

In our opinion, having a portfolio with only one type of investment isn't wise. Pouring all your money into new-company stocks, for example, is like putting your whole family in a hot air balloon and hoping everything will turn out OK. If all your money were invested in stocks, a financial crash would be devastating. And as you know, it has happened. That's why we split our investments between low- and high-risk vehicles. We agree on a given amount to invest in higher-risk investments. Our decisions on the amount are based on whether we could sleep at night and whether we could live normally financially even in the worst-case scenario.

Knowledge and a clear understanding of your investments are important. Research companies that interest you, know what returns your investment will most likely achieve and try to forecast the likelihood of it not producing as expected.

Our portfolio is spread across the following types of investments (in no specific order):

- High-risk individual stocks (in RRSPs and TFSAs)
- Mutual funds
- Real estate (principal home and rental properties)
- Individual first and second mortgages and MICs

To conclude, there's no perfect tool or strategy to measure risk. However, in our experience as investors, we have learned the value of diversifying and understanding the power of investing. Have we made

Chapter 9

mistakes along the way? Absolutely! With every mistake comes an important lesson, as you will see below when we discuss penny stocks, rental properties and real estate investments.

If you are an inexperienced investor, gauge your risk in terms of the odds that your investment will fail to achieve the expected return. Understand the extent to which it may miss that expected target. By understanding what risk is, and where it can come from, you can work to build a portfolio with a lower probability of loss. Always remember, if it's too good to be true, it probably is.

Real Estate

The average cost of a home in Toronto went from about $90,000 in 1980 to about $500,000 in 2014. During that time, house prices peaked in 1989 and then dropped until 1996, when they began to rise again. They've been steadily increasing ever since, although not at the dramatic rates seen during the late 1980s. Prices levelled off in 2008, but resumed their upward climb in 2009.

Here's what we experienced: We purchased our home in Richmond Hill, Ontario, just outside Toronto, in 2005 for $350,000. We sold it five years later for $589,000, gaining $239,000. After deducting legal and real estate fees and land transfer tax, we made a profit of approximately $200,000 in just five years.

The devil's advocate may ask how much interest we paid on our mortgage during those five years. Good question. Our amortization summary indicates that we paid approximately $52,000 in interest. If we had paid rent in the Greater Toronto Area on the same type of home, we would have paid about $2,100 per month. Over five years, that would equal $126,000 in rent, more than double what we paid in interest. In our opinion, paying interest – and having the opportunity to make a profit on selling the home – was far better than paying rent. So yes, we believe real estate is a good investment.

That said, renting a home or an apartment can also be a positive thing and is a great option for people who travel for long periods or who do contract work in different places. They can write off this expense through their business, saving them approximately 40% of the actual rental cost through the tax deduction. We have one tenant who runs a successful business out of the home he rents from us and writes off home and office expenses.

What are the risks of investing in real estate?

Good planning is essential when investing in a property: generate income by renting it out. This income will pay down the mortgage, reducing your debt and building equity.

There are risks, but let's have a look at the worst-case real estate scenario: You purchase a home for $350,000 with a 20% down payment of $70,000 and a mortgage of $280,000. In 10 years the house's value appreciates by $100,000 – your investment property is now worth $450,000 – and your tenants have paid off over one-third of the mortgage ($2,000 monthly rent × 12 months × 10 years = $240,000 in rental income). Now let's say 17 years after the purchase, your home is worth $550,000 and you have successfully paid off the mortgage with your rental income because you made accelerated payments. However, a year later, the housing market crashes and we enter a recession. On average, house prices fall $200,000, so your home is now worth $350,000 again. This is what you paid for it 17 years ago. You invested $70,000 (down payment only; the tenant paid the rest) and your net worth is now $350,000. Even in this worst-case scenario you are still very much ahead, coming out with about $280,000. This scenario is unlikely to play out, but it has happened – just ask our American neighbours. So if you believe real estate is not a good investment, think about that.

Another problem that can arise when you purchase property is that interest rates increase to levels where your rental income does not cover your mortgage payments and other bills. This scenario has to be part of your planning and you must be able to provide solutions.

As an investor, you must always consider worst-case scenarios to mitigate risk. Before investing in real estate ask yourself what you will do if

- You cannot find renters right away.
- A renter stops paying the rent.
- Interest rates go up substantially.
- An unforeseen major expenditure is required on the house (roof caves in, tree root blocks plumbing under house, weeping tile needs to be replaced around whole house, etc.).
- Insurance premiums go up dramatically.
- Utility costs (electricity or gas) go up.

The real estate crash that happened in the United States and many other countries left many landlords with properties they could not afford because they had purchased more than they could handle and had taken on too much debt. When the economy crashed and people started losing their jobs, they could no longer pay their rent, leaving landlords without the income needed to make payments on mortgages. So not only were renters losing their employment, so were their landlords.

As a general rule, make sure you have enough funds available to cover at least three months of payments for all your investment properties, either through salaries, savings such as a TFSA, a line of credit or a combination of these. If worse comes to worst, you have to be able to quickly sell your property. But before choosing that option, look at all possible ways to keep it and thus stay on track for meeting your goals.

Second Mortgage Investments

Second mortgage investments are the biggest reason we can live the way we do. Everything we did before we made these investments brought us to this stage. We are able to invest in second mortgages by using cash on hand and the equity from our real estate and yes, even with our RRSPs. We lend money at higher interest rates; the borrowers use their homes as collateral. This is the last ingredient of the formula that gives us the freedom to enjoy life to the fullest and be financially free.

We're asked a lot of questions about second mortgage investments: how secure are they? How much return do they yield? Is it difficult to get into this type of investment? There are three basic elements to a good second mortgage investment:

- The borrower's asset or collateral
- Your available cash
- The quality of the borrower

An **asset, or collateral,** is something pledged as security for a loan, to be forfeited in the event of a default. In our case, the property or project the money is borrowed for provides guaranteed value if the borrower does not make the payments. Property can be land, a condo, a townhome or a house. Money can also be borrowed for a project such as construction, a plaza, a mall or even a complex.

Cash is provided by you, the lender. It can be cash you have in your savings account or available through a line of credit based on the equity in your home. Recall that equity is the paid-for part of your home's value. Let's say your own home is worth $500,000 and you have a $200,000 mortgage on it. This means you have $300,000 of equity. Most banks will give you a HELOC of up to 80% of the full value of your home, minus your mortgage debt. In this case, you could have a $200,000 line of credit, giving you $200,000 to invest in second mortgages.

The borrower is the person or group looking to borrow your money. Your cash is lent against their assets, usually a home. Some may want to borrow this money for such things as renovations or paying off higher-interest debts such as credit card debt; it may be to invest in other real estate. We have one investor who borrowed to renovate his restaurant. There are many reasons people want to borrow money and because of tight regulations in our banking system, they don't qualify. They might have other debts and thus present a higher risk to the banks. However, we protect our investment by ensuring they have collateral to cover the funds we lend them.

Here's an example: The borrower has a home worth $500,000 and has a mortgage with a bank for $200,000. This mortgage is called a first mortgage. If you subtract the $200,000 first mortgage from the house value of $500,000, the borrower has $300,000 in equity in the home. Let's say the borrower wants to borrow $100,000 as a second mortgage from you for whatever reason. You now have to assess your risk. You do this by having the borrower's home evaluated by a reputable house appraiser. Once you determine that the home truly is worth $500,000, you go to the next step. You check the borrower's credit and debts and their primary source of income. You need to assess whether this person is responsible with their finances or whether they are in over their head. Lastly, you either go to see the property or closely study the appraiser's report. Study the location and pay attention to its surroundings because you want only prime real estate if you end up owning it.

Another important aspect for us when dealing with second mortgage investing is the length of the contract: we prefer one-year terms. This short-term approach mitigates the risks of real estate market fluctuations – it's impossible to accurately forecast what the economic situation will be five years from now or even two years from now. Therefore, we are more comfortable settling mostly one-year terms and renewing the mortgage if the borrower has respected all the agreement terms, never slipping into arrears. Once the borrower meets your expectations and criteria you can proceed with signing the commitment contract. Use a real estate lawyer to finalize the process.

What we like about this type of investing is the control we have over the process. We use our appraiser and our lawyer and we control the process from start to finish. On top of that, the lawyer's fees and administration fees are all paid by the borrower – we include this term in the agreement. There is no expense to us as the lenders. It is a win-win situation if you properly assess the investment.

Of course, when we started considering second mortgages, we had many questions; we wanted to know whether it was a secure investment. Let us illustrate with the following scenario. Let's say the borrower was not able to make the monthly payments. You as the lender have the option of foreclosure, or power of sale, forcing the sale of the collateral so that you can recover the money you lent. The down side of a foreclosure is that it can take up to a year to complete the process and the first mortgage lender, such as the bank, has first rights to collect their money. However, if you did your due diligence before finalizing the deal, you would have covered yourself by making sure the equity in the collateral home exceeded the amount you lent. In our example, the borrower has $300,000 in equity on a $500,000 house. This means there is still approximately $200,000 over and above the first mortgage debt ($200,000) and the $100,000 second mortgage debt. So when the house is sold, not only does the bank get its $200,000 and you get your $100,000 investment back, but you also get all the arrears in missed interest payments plus the penalty fees for every missed payment. So in the end you made more money with this defaulted deal than if the borrower had made all the payments on time.

When you look at this scenario, you can see that the last thing the borrower would want is to lose the $300,000 he or she has in equity, so the borrower is unlikely to default on payments. This assessment demonstrates the solidity of this type of investment.

We love this type of investing – it's our supplementary income and it allows us to live the life we do today. We credit our mortgage broker, Elie and his team for helping us discover second mortgage investing and for finding quality borrowers. For more information on second mortgages and Elie's team, go to *TheFortunateFew.com*.

Stocks

For us, investing in stocks is a bit like gambling. We are far from being experts in the subject, but the experiences we've had with this type of investment led us to that conclusion. In the short term, the behaviour of stock prices is based on rumours, lies, emotions and some factual news. In the long run, it is mainly company earnings that determine whether a stock's price will go up, down or sideways.

It may seem contradictory, because we consider stocks to be high-risk investments, but in all our research, stocks have proven to be a very good investment *over the long term*. Since World War II, despite crises and great volatility, with market crashes and surges, the average large-capitalization stock yielded a return of close to 10% yearly. This exceeds the rate of inflation and outperforms bonds, real estate and other types of investments. Many experts say stocks are the best investment if you stick to them for the long term.

When buying a stock, you are taking a share of ownership in a company. Collectively, the company is owned by all the shareholders. Each of these shares represents a claim on assets and earnings. A company might show great potential and prove to have a great track record but this does not guarantee its success in the future. Company stock prices are based on projections of future earnings. But buyer beware: even the highly successful companies can fall far. Think of RIM (now BlackBerry), for example.

Your stock portfolio planning should be for long-term growth and should include stocks from several different companies in different industries and even different parts of the world: diversify, diversify, diversify! Having all your eggs in one basket can be catastrophic.

"Penny stocks" in mining companies are notoriously risky. The majority of mining stocks fail, the companies never finding the needle in the haystack. People invest in them because of the small chance of incredible success. We know from experience that when it comes to mining stocks, there is a high chance of underperformance and that a large number of these companies simply fail, losing 95% or more of their value.

That said, any type of investment can fail and constant surveillance is needed if you invest in stocks. Remember Nortel? If you have the misfortune to invest in a company that goes bankrupt or becomes insolvent, you may be entitled to claim a capital loss. Your accountant will be able to assess whether you can claim a capital loss on your investment in a failed company. On the other hand, if you make money on your stocks, you will have to pay tax on that gain unless you are using funds inside a registered account (RRSP, TFSA).

An investor with all his or her money in one "low-risk" stock – all their eggs in one basket – is still playing with risk: in the event of a catastrophe for that one company, the investor's loss would be considerable. Spread your stock investments over five to 10 stocks of different kinds of companies to reduce the chances of a big loss. This is diversifying within your stock portfolio. The level of risk in your portfolio will decrease and stabilize: if one stock underperforms and a few others perform well, your overall portfolio will do fine.

Dividend-paying stocks might also be part of your plan to diversify your portfolio. Note that dividend-paying stocks of major Fortune 100 corporations are generally safe, and investors may be able to expect mid-to-high single-digit returns over the course of many years. That being said, crashes do occur. We never invested in Fortune 100 companies because we decided to go high risk with the stock portion of our portfolio.

The stock market is complicated and that's why many investors use a stock broker to help them make decisions about stock investments. Even with a broker, you have to remain involved because the only person in that equation truly working in your best interest is you. Stock brokers often sell products and packages promoted by their company and they collect a commission for selling these products. Also be aware of the fees brokers charge; they can be high. To avoid these fees, we opted for a self-directed account and we learned to manage our own investments. When we used a stock broker, buying or selling a stock cost us an average of $300 for every trade. Trades now cost us $14.95 in our self-directed account.

However, again, be aware: a self-directed account is exactly that. *You are responsible for everything pertaining to that account.* We had a problem with our self-directed account at one financial institution. We sent instructions to the institution that were not followed properly; the error cost us $5,000. The financial institution would not take responsibility because the account was self-directed and the bank felt we should have caught the error before it was submitted (the institution did, however, help us rectify the problem with the CRA and we did recover the $5,000). So when giving instructions for transactions within a self-directed account, be very clear and make sure your instructions are understood and followed.

As of July 15, 2014, Canadian brokerage firms are required to disclose the commission paid by their clients to buy or sell a bond or other fixed-income security. Additional reforms, called Client Relationship Model 2 (CRM 2), will continue to roll out through 2016 and are intended to bring more transparency to the investment industry. By 2016, disclosure of other fees, such as mutual fund deferred sales charges and trailer fees, will be required.

All investors should seek to understand the risks they are taking; how high fees, excessive portfolio turnover and unnecessary tax work against them; and how to avoid underperforming the market. The CRM 2 reforms will help you to know the cost of your investments, how your advisor is being compensated and what his or her return is after fees have been deducted. Regulators want consumers to focus on their statements and to ask more questions. Use the information you find there to arm yourself with knowledge, including what it costs to buy and sell bonds and other investments. Identify the weaknesses in your portfolio and address those issues.

Mortgage Investment Corporations

MICs are one of our favourite investment vehicles. A MIC is a company that allows lenders to pool their money to invest in mortgages. It is designed primarily for residential mortgage lending in Canada.

Investing

This means you are investing your money, with others, through a corporation in a variety of mortgages. You purchase shares in the corporation. These shares are qualified investments under the Canadian *Income Tax Act;* that is, they are recognized as legal. You can also invest in MICs inside your RRSP at some financial institutions; Olympia Trust and B2B are two that offer this.

Most MIC portfolios hold second mortgages on residential properties but they can also include commercial and development mortgages as well. The MIC we are involved with, called Cannect, includes a lot of development mortgages in which even borrowers have their own money invested in their projects. The team that manages this fund always does its due diligence to assure investors that the borrowers are in good standing and have a good track record. As a general rule, the managers never allow the potential client to borrow in excess of 60% to 80% of the current value of the property or project. The MIC team normally does a thorough investigation of the property, including a professional appraisal, legal review and credit check on the borrower.

Every MIC is different, so do your homework and make sure you invest in one you are comfortable with. We insist on having a top-notch team managing the fund in addition to top-quality investments. Most MICs will generate returns between 6% and 12%. Returns do vary based on the strategy used by the individual MIC. Make sure you look at the terms of your investment because if you wish to pull out of the fund early, there will be a penalty. Normally you need to stay with the investment for a set term; ours is five years.

Profits made within the pool are distributed evenly among all shareholders (investors) according to the percentage of their investment. The investment is secured against the value of the property being mortgaged and sometimes the borrower is required to add other forms of security, such as their business, cottage or other assets.

Chapter 9

Like most investments, there is risk in MICs, both management risk, such as mistakes or poor decisions by the management team, and real estate market risk, such as a drastic drop in property values. One important element of MICs, however, is that any losses are shared by all investors.

Not every MIC is transparent – in other words, you don't get all the details about every borrower. This information is held only by the team managing this fund. We insist on transparency and Cannect does exactly that, making this information available to its investors.

For more information on the Cannect MIC go to *TheFortunateFew.com*.

A Few Fortunate Thoughts about Investing

- Pay off bad debt before you start investing. This should be within the first couple of years of your 10-year plan.
- From our perspective, very few types of investments yield the return produced with real estate, especially when a market correction or crash occurs. For us, real estate is a secure investment. Do your homework, study the market and pick prime locations.
- Invest in second mortgages. Banks make money because they sell products that generate guaranteed returns and they secure their loans with their customers' assets. Capitalize on this idea – it's one of the keys to our freedom.
- Be aware that investing in stocks is like gambling. Pick a casino with less risk. Consider dividend-paying stocks in a well-diversified portfolio. Do your research and find companies that have good reputations and track records. Studies show that stocks are an excellent long-term investment.
- Understand that MICs are only as good as the team running them. Look carefully at the product and the borrowers they lend to. Get to know the team running the corporation. Being part of a pool of investors is a great way to mitigate your investment risk.
- Select investment vehicles you are comfortable with after assessing your risk tolerance. Diversify to protect your portfolio from negative outcomes. Spread out your investment portfolio by having your money in many different investments.

Summary

The future depends on what you do today.
Gandhi

Summary

A family trip to Italy

Carole

Venice is unlike any other town. No matter how many times you have seen it in movies or on TV, the real thing is more surreal and dreamlike than you ever imagined. When our son, Corey, turned 16, we decided to travel to Europe, the three of us, each with a backpack and a wish list of things to see, eager for adventure. We had not overly planned this trip: no hotels were booked and no transportation was pre-arranged. We landed in Rome and slowly made our way to the other side of the "boot" of Italy to see the Adriatic Sea – and to discover the floating city.

You must walk almost everywhere in Venice and where you cannot walk, you go by water. Sunlight shimmers and silvery mist envelops the city in the morning, a fairy tale of canals and breathtaking architecture. At sunset, Venice is full of secrets, ineffably romantic, and – at times – given over entirely to pleasure. Daniel and I had planned a romantic walk through the city at night. On the second day, after a peaceful first night's sleep in the city and getting acquainted with our quarters, we asked Corey if he wanted to join us. He replied, "No, I think I will just stay here and chill; you won't be long." We understood as it had been a long day.

We swiftly took off into the night, following in the footsteps of Casanova, exploring the sites of his amorous adventures. Venice was far from being asleep, with thousands of lanterns beaming on the water, lighting up the wavelets like the facets of a diamond. We walked hand in hand along one of the many routes leading to Piazza San Marco. The experience was surreal: not only the lights but also the sounds were amplified, sounding off the stone walls and travelling across the shinning surface of the water. We could clearly hear multiple conversations through kitchen windows and hotel halls. It reminded us of studying The Merchant of Venice in high school. We fully understood how centuries ago spies walked the city at night, from one windowsill to the next, gathering secrets.

We strolled along a row of restaurants, where patrons were having dinner, laughing and talking loudly, surrounded by the aromas of garlic, tomatoes and grilled food. We found a quiet corner, close to a small marina, and leaned on a wide whitewashed bridge post. Daniel took me in his arms and we embraced and kissed. I felt my whole body rocking gently, like the small vaporetti boats next to us. The picture on the cover of this book celebrates that moment. We

Summary

gazed into each other's eyes, our hands looking for warmth, feeling the contours of our bodies, as if sculpting. We kissed again, and for a moment, forgot about the exquisiteness of the scenery around us, feeling only the intensity of our eternal love, as if it were our last kiss. For that moment, I was Juliet and Daniel was my Romeo.

A moment to remember, Venice, Italy

Summary

Our son, Corey, is in his early twenties and already an avid traveller. Like us, he learns so much as he travels and now that he has his first full-time job, he is planning to go to Cuba for a romantic trip with his sweetheart.

He is also asking more questions about investing because he would love to own a home. He has been a witness to every step we took to be among the fortunate few: every house we bought, every tenant we had, every weekend and evenings we worked and every meeting we had with our broker. He also dreams of retiring early to enjoy all life has to offer. He too must have a 10-year plan pinned up in his apartment!

Summary

Join the Fortunate Few!

As we write this summary, we are having a glass of wine in a café in Mijas Pueblo – a white village perched on the mountains overlooking the Mediterranean Sea in Spain. In the distance we can see the Strait of Gibraltar and Morocco – perhaps calling us for our next adventure.

This book retraced our journey to this point – investing in our first home, the right and wrong decisions, the sound and risky investments we made and how, with a clear plan, we stayed on track and retired at 45. We've also shared our financing and investment principles, which were key to our success – they guided our decisions and reflect the values we have tried to instill in our son. We wanted to inspire you to dream by sharing our own adventures, travels and magical moments. After all, what are life and freedom if you don't know what to do with them and have no one to share them with?

We shared our story to show you that you can achieve whatever you want in life. Reach your goals. Yes, there are obstacles, but with determination, perseverance, motivation, willpower and, above all, a positive outlook, you can attain anything you wish. Life is short – we are all chasing dreams and a sense of freedom. As Canadians we are lucky to live in a country that allows us to freely pursue our hopes and aspirations.

Love life, embrace the possibilities offered to you every day and plan. Don't let the media persuade you that you are forever young – there's a time for everything in life and some things you have to tackle sooner rather than later. Do it now while your are able; health is the key to everything.

Your journey to financial freedom can be roughly divided into three phases. We provide a brief summary below. We made it in 10 years, starting with writing out a plan, then acquiring our first home together in 2003 and finally quitting our jobs at the end of 2012.

Summary

It begins with the way you think

- Life is what you make it. If you feel stuck or are unhappy with any aspect of your life – job, relationship, finances – take action to change it. You may need to step out of your comfort zone and make some difficult decisions. You have the power to transform yourself.
- Think about the lifestyle you want. What are your expectations? What do you want to do with your time? Now think about how much money your truly need to achieve those goals.
- Think of your goals in terms of the pleasure they will bring, not in terms of the pain it may take to get there.
- Determine what financial independence means to you.
- Understand that living within your means must become a central tenet of your life. Differentiate your wants from your needs.
- Understand that you must take responsibility for looking after your own financial future.
- Educate yourself: read about all aspects of finance and investing and about setting and achieving goals.

It continues with planning

- Embrace the to-do list – it will keep you organized as you work toward your goals.
- Time management is critical. Automate or delegate everything you can in your life to save time, allowing you to focus on what matters.
- Analyze your life for time-wasting activities and eliminate them.
- Create realistic, detailed, short- and long-term plans, such as our one-, two-, three-, five- and 10-year plans. Keep them updated. And follow them!

Summary

- Build a team of experts to help you achieve your goals, including partners if you need them. You need people who understand your vision, who will help you make better decisions and who will make it easier for you to attain your goals.

It really is about money

- Pay off all "bad" debt such as credit card balances and vacation loans.
- Develop a plan for paying off other debt, including your mortgage, as quickly as possible.
- Track your spending and income, and then make a realistic budget and stick to it.
- Follow our formula for success, or develop your own, until you're earning enough through investments to quit your job:
    - Save at least 10% of your net income to purchase a home – maximize your RRSPs and TFSAs.
    - Build equity and use its power to invest.
    - Purchase investment properties to rent out using the Smith Manoeuvre.
    - Invest in diverse vehicles, including second mortgages and MICs.
- Do thorough research before investing in anything, on both the prospective investment and the people involved – if it sounds too good to be true, it likely is.

We hope this book empowers you and gives you the drive it takes to attain the freedom you desire. In the end, only you can bring yourself to be among the fortunate few – good luck!

References

Psychology Today
http://www.psychologytoday.com/blog/the-real-story-risk/201211/the-thing-we-fear-more-death

Zig Ziglar Newsletter
http://www.ziglar.com/newsletter/july-14-2009-edition-27

Creative Conflict Solutions
http://creative-conflict-solutions.com/2014/08/10/create-your-best-life-planning-beyond-goals/

Statistics Canada, Average Income after Tax by Economic Family Types
http://www.statcan.gc.ca/tables-tableaux/sum-som/l01/cst01/famil21a-eng.htm

Canadian Mortgage and Housing Corporation regulations for first home buyers
https://www.cmhc-schl.gc.ca/en/index.cfm

Canadian Bankers Association, Credit Cards: Statistics and Facts
http://www.cba.ca/en/media-room/50-backgrounders-on-banking-issues/123-credit-cards

Other Resources

Web resources
www.TheFortunateFew.com
http://www.thefortunatefew.com/tools-and-resources/

http://www.morcandirect.com/
http://www.customizemymortgage.ca
http://online-homes.net/

Compound interest calculator
http://mortgageintelligence.ca/mi/calculators/renewing-calculators/mortgage-calculator/

Mortgage loan calculator
https://www.morcandirect.com/calculators

References

How long to be a millionaire calculator
http://www.bankrate.com/calculators/savings/saving-million-dollars.aspx?MSA=&MSA=&MSA=&MSA=

Jump start your retirement plan
https://www.nbcmore.ca/investmenttrack/retraite/comprendre/?gclid=CLyN8Lyh774CFYhAMgodNgYAzg

Service Canada
http://www.servicecanada.gc.ca

Canada Revenue Agency
http://www.cra-arc.gc.ca/menu-eng.html

Books

Kiyosaki, Robert T., with Sharon L. Lechter. *Rich Dad, Poor Dad: What the Rich Teach Their Kids About Money That the Poor and Middle Class Do Not!* Warner Business Books, 1997.

Robbins, Anthony. *Unlimited Power: The New Science of Personal Achievement.* Pocket Books, 2001.

Robbins, Anthony. *Awaken the Giant Within: How to Take Immediate Control of Your Mental, Emotional, Physical and Financial Life.* Pocket Books, 2001.

Robbins, Anthony. *Personal Power II audio series.* Robbins Research International, 1996.

Smith, Fraser. *The Smith Manoeuvre: Is Your Mortgage Tax Deductible?* Outspan, 2005.

Magazines

MoneySense (http://www.moneysense.ca/)

Acknowledgements

Donna Dawson
Elie Soberano
Marcus Tzaferis
Rose Winkworth
Jana & Josie Zocco

Daniel

Carole is the reason for my happiness. She is the centre of my world and has been the strength behind everything we do. I continue to admire her wisdom and professionalism every day and I see these same qualities in Corey, my son. I try to implement her approach in my own life.

My mother, Denise, is a strong intellectual; she has always been an inspiration. Her strongest words of wisdom are forever engraved in my mind: *tout fini par s'arranger* – in time, things will work out.

My father, Jeannot, taught me entrepreneurial skills. He beat all odds and I learned determination to succeed from him. I will remain forever grateful. You can find his story at *TheFortunateFew.com.*

My brother, Michel, is the kindest and most generous man I know. He is my twin and I love him very much.

I owe much of our success to James Campbell, a lifelong friend who introduced me to the to-do list and made me aware of the endless possibilities life has to offer. As James says, "keep living the dream!"

Réal Pilon taught me the meaning of selflessness. Although he was my supervisor for a long time, he treated me as he would his brother. He has encouraged me throughout my career and I owe him my gratitude.

Acknowledgements

Carole

My thanks to my parents, Robert and Liette, who made sure all of us – six children – never lacked anything, especially love and attention. We often brag about how rich we are, not in the financial sense but because all of us are healthy and living in harmony, peace and love. I love my family and remain profoundly grateful. Papa and Maman are still the best model I have for a loving and caring relationship: they are still in love after 60 years of marriage.

My thanks also to Daniel, whom I love with all my heart and who generated the concepts for this book, persistently working away every morning for the past year. He stands as the motor behind this project. I keep learning from him every day and thank Providence for making it possible for us to meet. Daniel has also enriched my life with the most precious gift – Corey, who is a beautiful soul and of whom I am so proud.

I was blessed with a wonderful career and loved every job I had. I have been surrounded by people who believed in me and inspired me to reach my full potential. I remain grateful and feel it's now my turn to give back.

We feel a lot of gratitude as we think about the people we have met and worked with over the years. Some remain close friends and we still cherish the memory of those who have continued on a different path. All were important parts of our journey. Our past is what makes us what we are today and we believe we would not be where we are and who we have become if it hadn't been for the people who influenced us on a very personal level.